SONG,

Courage.

XEALOTS

love,

Other Books by Dave Gibbons

The Monkey and the Fish

X E A L O T S

defying the gravity of normality

DAVE GIBBONS

ZONDERVAN®

ZONDERVAN.com/
AUTHORTRACKER
follow your favorite authors

ZONDERVAN

Xealots
Copyright © 2011 by Dave Gibbons

This title is also available as a Zondervan ebook. Visit www.zondervan.com/ebooks.

This title is also available in a Zondervan audio edition. Visit www.zondervan.fm.

Requests for information should be addressed to:

Zondervan, *Grand Rapids, Michigan* 49530

Library of Congress Cataloging-in-Publication Data

Gibbons, Dave, 1962 –
    Xealots : defying the gravity of normality / Dave Gibbons.
       p.   cm.
    Includes bibliographical references
    ISBN 978-0-310-32702-8 (softcover)
    1. Christian life. 2. Conformity. I. Title.
BV4509.5.G467 2011
248.4 – dc22   2011015982

Published in association with Yates & Yates, www.yates2.com.

Cover design: PlainJoe Studios
Cover photography: Big Stock Photo
Interior illustration: Johnny Davis
Interior design: Sherri L. Hoffman

Printed in the United States of America

11 12 13 14 15 16 /DCI/ 22 21 20 19 18 17 16 15 14 13 12 11 10 9 8 7 6 5 4 3 2 1

To my children,
Leigh, Karis, Luke, and Megan

I wrote this book with you in mind. I wanted to share some thoughts that have guided me over the years. Our challenge is often to separate what is expected of us from what God invites us into. It's not so much about finding a job as it is about experiencing your God. My hope is that you will live in Narnia every day, fully awake, fully present, and wholly engaged in a beautiful world filled with adventure. I pray you will gain boldness to live your lives without fear.

With gratitude:

Thanks to the company of 300 XEALOTS who are comrades and great friends. As Bill Hwang says, "We're in the family business." You helped to make this book come alive.

Rebecca, Jimmy Lee, Eric, Dave Brubaker, Bill and Becky Hwang, Adam Edgerly, Darryl Brumfield, the Newsong family, the City on a Hill family in NYC, Aeran Moon, Sam Oh, Jaeson Ma, Carl Choi, Mike Wang, Tom and Diane Greer, Bronnie Lee, Cue Jean Marie, and Jim Gustafson.

Love you all!

CONTENTS

INTRODUCTION

imagine

TWO questions.

First: if the evil forces of the universe strategized to paralyze the most potent force on earth, who would they target?

I believe they'd target you.

You have unbelievable potential. Sure, we're all flawed. We can be erratic. We can be addictive. We can be self-centered. We can be, frankly, odd.

Yet you are the apple of God's eye. A supernatural favor is your inheritance. It's in your gene pool. You can't run away from it. Your destiny is to see the unleashing of beauty through miracles, dreams, and visions. You're part of the rising tide of God's church. You are living in one of the most thrilling seasons in history.

At the same time, you face challenges. You live in a world where it's hard to listen. It's hard to pay attention. It's normal to focus only on what you can see.

Second: how would these evil forces keep you from your destiny? Their scheme is covert. The enemy wants you to think you're doing something significant, when in reality you may be doing nothing at all.

You may be practicing a form of godliness without the power.

Can you hear it?[1]

A song is playing in your heart right now. It has a defiant beat. It provokes rebellion, the feeling in your gut that something isn't right with the way you're living. It's a hunch inside you. It whispers, "You weren't meant for the 'normal' life." Everyone around you thinks you have it great, but you know there's something more. You were meant to live with a zealous, radical belief in the supernatural power of God. You were designed to unleash beauty. But the status quo induces a mesmerizing, trancelike state. People walk around distracted, captivated by the superficial, ignorant of what is real, of eternal value. You must take a stand when gravitational forces try pulling you down.

This book is about an abnormal flow to life, a positive defiance of what popular culture accepts. It's about a holy rebellion. A XEALOT lives according to contrarian principles. A XEALOT swims against the tide. I pray that as you read, you'll sense the galvanizing of a positive defiance within you. It stands up in the face of criticism, not dazzled by cultural idols or transfixed by the lullaby of comfort. My hope is that you become countercultural, yet adaptive to culture. It's an art that requires a radical obedience to the Holy Spirit's leading in your life. It's a life that is supernaturally natural.

I don't believe we're necessarily supposed to reject or transform culture. Our calling is to wisely flow with culture, guarding our hearts and minds, artfully engaging our world. Transforming people's hearts is the work of God. Our mission is to be loving instruments of change. If God wills, he is the one who changes culture. However, there are times when we must be positively defiant when culture attempts to shape us to forces contrary to God.

My hope is that as you read this mosaic of musings, you'll feel an excitement, a stirring, a call to a peculiar path for your life. The way of those who follow Christ defies the gravity of normality. It's the way of the fool. It's an act of rebellion. Though many might not follow you, you're called to this crazy adventure. You come from a line of immigrant tribes, misfits, marginalized clans, invisible creatives, and unknown explorers. You're a radical crew of XEALOTS God has raised all over the world.

Defy normality.

PART 1

MIND

The minds on the margins aren't marginal minds.

— ANIL GUPTA

Nelson Mandela

OFF THE coast of Cape Town, South Africa, a defunct penitentiary called Robben Island stands between the mountains and the sea. This is the prison that once held anti-apartheid activist Nelson Mandela.

In the prison's later days, most of the inmates were young and black, or "colored," typically of mixed race or of Indian descent. The guards were young and white. To keep the inmates occupied during their long hours of captivity, the guards ordered them to move gravel from one hole in the ground to another. It was labor without a purpose. Mandela, though twenty years older than most of the other prisoners, was forced to daily engage in this work. While his body was occupied with pointless labor, however, his mind remained free. During his long years of imprisonment on the island, Mandela transformed the lime quarry into an institution of higher learning.

When Mandela was young, Methodist missionaries in South Africa ignited a passion in his heart. It was a passion for freedom. The education he received gave him a radical view of divine grace. His understanding of the power of forgiveness grew. The things he studied as a boy taught him a contrarian way of life. During his time on Robben Island, Mandela turned his mind into a portal. His mind was a land where he could explore revolutionary ideas. The freedom of his mind not only helped him to maintain his sanity behind the gray concrete slabs; it helped him create beauty in the midst of his confinement. With each shovelful of gravel they transported, Mandela and his cohorts were in "school." Mandela shared the things he had learned from his missionary education: Shakespeare, the Scriptures, the great poets and philosophers, the ancient Bantu wisdom of *Umuntu, ngumeutu ngabantu* ("We are people through other people"), as well as what he knew of Jesus' and Gandhi's views on reconciliation. Robben Island soon became Robben Island University. Mandela arranged secret lectures focused on teaching the prisoners their need for one another. He taught them that common ground is greater than the differences that divide. He showed them that while people can control and abuse our bodies, they cannot control our minds.

If our minds remain free, regardless of our circumstances, we can live free.

Most of the wisdom literature of the Bible was penned by a man named Solomon. King Solomon wrote hundreds of proverbs, short sayings that summarize timeless truths. In one of his proverbs, Solomon wrote this simple phrase: "As a man thinks in his heart, so he becomes."

Our beliefs determine how we live. Our actions and feelings emerge out of our beliefs. All of us will likely have experiences that bring us to a state of physical, emotional, or spiritual exhaustion. Unexpected catastrophe can cause personal collapse. But in challenging times, disciplined minds defy the conformity to a culture of discontent. The mind is the vehicle that enables us to transcend oppression.

We see this proven in sporting venues week after week. It's the end of the game with seconds remaining on the clock. A basketball player stands at the free throw line. His veins are bulging. His blood is pumping vigorously. Horns are blowing around him. Fans of the opposing team are waving their arms, trying to distract him. Even with his athleticism, he suddenly loses confidence. He misses the shot.

But the elite athlete knows the secret of winning. He lives in another realm. He blocks out the loud voices of the crowd. He knows how to play in "the zone," a protected space of mental concentration. To win the battle on the basketball court, he first wins the battle in his mind.

This focus is the art of seizing the opportunity. It's about muting the voices that frighten us. God's voice takes over and we lose ourselves in the moment. We do what God is calling us to do in spite of adversity.

Life is filled with opportunities to live out God's calling. How we develop our minds prepares us for those divine adventures. There is a status quo way of thinking that leads to distraction. And there is a contrarian way that leads to life. It may not lead to a life of material abundance. The path does lead to joy. The secret to experiencing this joy is learning to defy the gravitational pull of our culture's values. In this defiance, XEALOTS simultaneously construct a mind of wisdom.

In the New Testament letter of the apostle Paul to the Romans, Paul lays out a doctrinal treatise on the grace of God. Near the conclusion of his teaching, he implores his readers to live as people of grace: "And so, dear brothers and sisters, I plead with you to give your bodies to God because of all he has done for you. Let them be a living and holy sacrifice — the kind he will find acceptable. This is truly the way to worship him. Don't copy the behavior and customs of this world, but let God transform you into a new person by changing the way you think. Then you will learn to know God's will for you, which is good and pleasing and perfect."[1]

The grace-filled life is a contrarian life, a positive defiance, the life of a person who doesn't "copy the behavior and customs of this world." And this happens by "changing the way you think."

In part 1 of this book, we'll examine axioms that shape the XEALOT's mind. These are meditations that produce wisdom. They are meant to be not an exhaustive set of beliefs but an important beginning. Out of these core rhythms of the mind come life and peace. These core contrarian truths are remixed for a new wave of XEALOTS.

Letting the Spirit control your mind leads to life and peace.
— ROMANS 8:6

1

ZOMBIES
the problem with normality

IMAGINE walking down the tree-lined street of a typical, suburban neighborhood. We stop to look into several of the windows. Peering into the interiors of the houses, and what do we see? In most homes, the scene is identical: families huddled around a flat screen, nonconversant, fixated on the pixels. Each clan is lulled into a mindless slumber. We have become a society medicating our boredom. We are distracted. We are asleep.

Suppose we stroll to a local school. There we find young people bored out of their minds. To generate excitement in their lives, the younger ones use video games. The older adolescents turn to alcohol and designer drugs for a cheap high. But soon, the batteries wear out and the high fades. Entertainment and the pursuit of pleasure leads to a nightmare of addictions, arrests, failed relationships, and excuses. Soon these young people become part of the multitude of "zombies," the living dead who are caught in a cycle of consumption. The cravings of their souls go unsatiated.

Now let's walk to the business buildings where the "successful" people spend their time. Here too we see people in the doldrums. Millions are feeling trapped by the predictable nature of their daily lives. It's the same routine every day. They medicate by keeping occupied, staring at some screen or another. An illusion of productivity is projected. Outside of the office, they zone out by cranking the volume on their car stereos.

This is normality. This is the life most of us live. It's the natural way.

This is the socially acceptable way to live. We choose the path of least resistance to flow with the crowd. Part of the masses, we drink our fake elixirs to numb reality.

Normality is a seductive trap, one we can easily fall prey to if we're not vigilant. We don't start out thinking, "I want to be normal when I grow up." Most of us begin life with dreams and ambitions. We have hopes inspired in us by parents and teachers, mentors and coaches. "We will change the world" becomes "I just have to get through today." Yet little by little, we are hypnotized by the normal life. We become entangled by distractions. We swallow the illusions of decadence. We are spoon-fed, afraid to take risks. Normal becomes our default lifestyle. We

find ourselves in a rut, eyes half open. We forget that we were made for something more. Each of us has a destiny. Jesus once said that few will find this destiny, this narrow path. It's not the wide, well-lit road that many take. It's an unnatural path, the road less traveled.

WHAT IS NORMAL?

When you look at the normal life, it doesn't really make much sense. If you are normal,

- you do stuff because you feel like it.
- you sleepwalk through routines.
- you live for the weekend.
- you talk about your future and live in the past.
- you treat people as a means to accomplish your goals.
- your image doesn't really match who you know yourself to be.
- titles, things, and achievements fuel your sense of worth.
- you yearn for intimacy, but few people actually know you.
- you never have enough.

Our lives are filled with noise. We are surrounded by people and endlessly entertained. We have little real connection to life. We create illusions. Like the drone of a treadmill, our lives acquire a static state that douses the fire in our hearts. This is the American dream. Filled with glitzy promises, ultimately this is a life that is devoid of meaning or eternal purpose. And it's not only those who are lured by Western culture who walk this path. This is the common path walked by the human race, the normal flow that leads to destruction.

There has to be something more.

We all know that people don't fly. We aren't birds. We don't have wings. We are subject to the restraints of gravity; it keeps us grounded. And this is a good thing. Gravity gives us a sense of stability and security. We can depend on it, knowing that what goes up must always come down.

But what if something happened — something unusual — that allows us to defy gravity? What if human beings were able to grow wings? What if we could fly, pushing against the earth's gravitational pull?

It would be unprecedented.

Phenomenal.

Abnormal.

I'm drawn to people with eccentricities. Some would call them unusual. I call them fascinating. They walk to a different beat. They are not concerned with popular opinion. Abnormal people give a stale world a burst of flavor. They add color to a black-and-white palette. They illuminate spaces that are otherwise dark. And that's exactly what Jesus wanted of his own disciples. Jesus described his followers as the salt and light of the world. Jesus knew that they add spice to a bland world. These defiant ones reflect the light of God in the darkness of normality. The great news is that no one is disqualified from living this extraordinary life. Anyone can become a rebel against the norm. It doesn't matter what your story is or what town you came from.

My friend has a T-shirt that reads, "It's Okay to Like Math." This shirt is really an invitation to come out from whatever hole you are hiding in. Just be you! It's okay to be weird.

Embrace your peculiarity. It's what makes you unique.

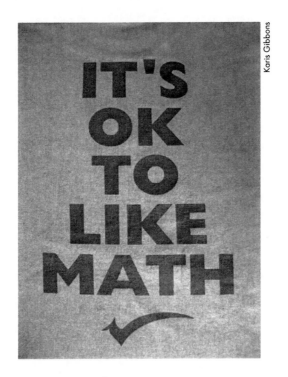

Karis Gibbons

I recently had the chance to talk to Ralph Winter about the importance of being abnormal. I wondered what does it look like to develop a habit of abnormality? Winter is the producer of the blockbuster trilogy of X-Men movies. Both the original comic book story line and the recent Hollywood movies convey the story of superheroes who have been rejected by the world. The X in their name refers to their possession of an "X gene," a gene that normal human beings lack. Their abnormalities give these mutants their extraordinary abilities. Considered freaks by the regular people, the X-Men are treated with suspicion, scorn, and hatred.

And yet the mutation that makes them different from the average person proves to be an amazing gift. One of the senior

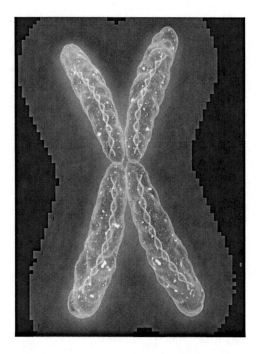

mutants, Professor Xavier, creates a haven at his Westchester mansion to nurture the gifts of the mutants to benefit all of humanity. It is the very qualities that make the X-Men abnormal that end up saving the world—countless times. Their abnormality is a superpower that can change the world.

As I talked with Ralph about the story line of his movies, we both agreed: this is a true story, one that resonates with our experience. We talked about the need for a haven similar to the one created by Professor Xavier, a place where those who live on the fringe—the "mutants" and abnormals of our culture—can find a place of safety, a place where their gifts and ideas are nurtured, a sanctuary where abnormalities are regarded as a means to change the world.

Many years ago, I started XEALOT, an organization designed to serve as a "special ops" type of human development program. XEALOT equips and affirms the special destinies of misfit-type leaders from around the globe. I chose the name XEALOT because I was thinking of the term *zealot*, a person who is passionate about an idea or a cause. A XEALOT is willing to die for what he believes in. I spelled it with an X instead of a Z as an allusion to the Greek letter *chi* (X), an abbreviation for *Christ*. XEALOTS believe that through the power of Jesus Christ, ordinary men and women can develop "superhuman" abilities to change the world. XEALOT leaders are lovers and learners committed to advancing the cause of Christ. From a societal perspective, they are severely flawed. They are not your normal superheroes, chosen from the gene pool of the world's brightest and best. They are commonly in the hidden spaces of our world. They are misfits with a supernatural destiny.

We live in a world that is comfortable with stereotypes. We place people in neat boxes according to ethnicity, economic status, appearance, and education. Those who meet our standard of normality are acceptable. They fit our expectations. They meet with our approval. But if we sense any hint of deformity, capital lack, ugliness, or a questionable past without distinction, we label them freaks, handicapped, and even aliens.

When we look at Jesus, we discover that he didn't fit the normal mold. He came from a town with a lowly reputation: "Can anything good come from that wrong-side-of-the-tracks town called Nazareth?" a cynic once asked.[1] Jesus emerged from the margins. Jesus also had some questionable women in his family tree: an adulteress named Bathsheba, a woman on welfare named Ruth, and a prostitute named Rahab. On top of all of this, Jesus' own birth was marred by gossip and rumor because he was born to a teenage virgin. Jesus failed to meet his culture's standard of acceptability.

But his outcast past became his connection to humanity. People relate to his pain. His life is a reminder that God is in the margins. He embraces the shame of our sinful history. God turns it into good. Those who are weighed down by the baggage of mistakes or who lack the credentials of normality discover new hope in Jesus. Jesus leads the way.

FREAKS

We are all gifted. Often I've found that our unique gifts, the ones that free us to be used by God most powerfully, are our weaknesses. God's strength is made perfect in our weakness.

Far too often, though, we try to bury our weaknesses. We see them as abnormalities that people shouldn't see. We cover up the parts of our lives that seem weird, freakish, or offbeat. The parts that make us beautifully unique, we hide. Instead, we showcase our strengths. We strive to prove that we are just as good as everyone else. We highlight the things that make us acceptable in the eyes of the world. We inflate the things that normal people applaud. We become good at creating facades. We develop a habit of projecting an inflated image.

What a waste of time.

Normal people spend their lives walking on the ground, but God calls us to defy gravity. If it's abnormal to have wings, so be it. I'd rather fly than walk. The Scriptures tell us that "the stone that the builders rejected has now become the corner-stone. This is the LORD's doing, and it is wonderful to see."[2] It was the very thing that people thought disqualified Jesus from being sent by God that ended up being the reason he succeeded. What looked like a failure in the eyes of the world was actually a success in the eyes of his heavenly Father.

You've heard people—particularly after a really bad day— say, "That's the story of my life."

"So I'm on my way to that job interview and I get a flat tire. Story of my life."

"I just missed my appointment, and now I have to wait another five weeks. Story of my life."

People exaggerate like this, suggesting that their lives are a never-ending string of bad luck, failure, and mistakes, in order to make a point. But I think that this saying accurately reflects the story of Jesus' life, and of the lives of many of the heroes of the Christian faith. The story line of God's people throughout the Bible is one of failure and intense suffering. God rarely chooses the successful or the gifted. He seems to pick the last person anyone would ever want on their team.[3]

Instead of choosing those who are brilliant in the eyes of the world, God chooses the people the world considers foolish—the freaks and the mutants—in order to shame those who think they are wise.[4] God can use anyone, but when he chooses to use us, it often isn't our strengths or gifts that make us useful for his purposes.

It's our weaknesses.

Our abnormalities.

The things that make us different connect us to most of the world.

And the things that make us misfits give us the gift of flight.

MUTANT SEEDS

Norm Ozawa is an amazingly humble Japanese-American. Tanned, muscular, and stocky, Norm is filled with life. His occupation is planting seeds and growing plants. For years he

has nurtured his nurseries in the fertile valleys of Southern California.

Norm handles thousands of seeds and tenderly cares for them. He says that on occasion a mutant seed will appear, one that is different. This seed is indistinguishable until it grows into a plant. Norm says this mutant plant is extremely valuable. When he finds one, he separates it from the other plants. Then he sets a team to work at reproducing it. Why? Because the mutation is nature's way of preparing this family of seeds for the challenges of their changing environment. It's nature's and God's gift to us.

I thought about Norm and his seeds. I realized that Jesus too is mutant-like. He is unique, yet ordinary. In the beginning of time, a seed was planted through the line of Adam and his family. But soon after, the environment changed. The earth grew cold, the sky darkened, and human sinfulness brought about a fallen world. A new seed had to be born so that the human race could survive these new conditions.

Jesus is that seed. He is the original mutant seed. He is the connection to life. The Scriptures tell us that there was nothing physically attractive about him. Jesus wouldn't have caught our eye.

There is immeasurable value in a different kind of seed.

Do you feel unusual? Abnormal? Do you know you're like a mutant? Well, you're in good company. There's a reason why you are this way. You have a destiny to fulfill that is anything but ordinary. God is using you to give life.

2

CHUANG TZU

perceptions of God, ourselves,
others, and our work

When Christ calls a man, he bids him come and die. that
is why the rich young man was so loath to follow Jesus, for
the cost of his following was the death of his will. In fact,
every command of Jesus is a call to die, with all our affec-
tions and lusts.

— DIETRICH BONHOEFFER, *THE COST OF DISCIPLESHIP*

IN HIS book *The Three Christs of Ypsilanti*, psychologist Mil-
ton Rokeach describes his interaction with three men who each
believed they were the living incarnation of God. To help these
three individuals learn to deal with their mistaken self-percep-
tions, he placed them into a support group.

Putting three self-proclaimed messiahs into the same room
made for some interesting conversations. One of the men started
the discussion with a bold statement. "I want you all to know
I'm the Son of God."

Rokeach asked, "Who told you that?"

The man responded with absolute certainty, "God did."

At this, one of the other men, with equal confidence, corrected him: "I never told you that before."

We all have illusions.

Our perceptions, whether clear or distorted, shape our reality. Contemplative Parker Palmer has said there are four perceptions that guide the way we think and behave:

1. Our perception of God
2. Our perception of ourselves
3. Our perception of others
4. Our perception of our work

Our perceptions have such power. The Scriptures warn us to guard the beliefs that shape our hearts: "Guard your heart above all else, for it determines the course of your life."[1] The beliefs that we hold most deeply shape and determine who we are and the way we live. Our beliefs ultimately become the foundation of our behavior. Beliefs spark and sustain movements in our lives. Let's look at these four areas of belief.

GOD: ABUNDANCE OR SCARCITY?

Our understanding of God shapes our identity. He inspires our actions. If you view God as one who favors you, your perspective likely will be one of abundance, regardless of your circumstances. Because you know that your heavenly Father wants to ridiculously bless you with every good and perfect gift, your love will generously overflow toward others. The abundance I am referring to is more than a material overflow. It's a quality of existence. A healthy understanding of who God is will lead to a qualitatively better life. Some questions to wrestle with are:

How do I see God? Do I live in fear of God? Am I constantly seeking his favor, living to earn his approval? Do I bask in his extravagant love? Does his love empower and change the way I live?

If you tend to see God as distant, reluctant to release his generosity, you probably have developed a lifestyle that is centered on preservation. It's easy, then, to become risk averse. You may find you are constantly anxious, worried about not having enough resources. You see the world through a lens of scarcity. Take a moment to compare your perception with what Jesus teaches in Matthew 7:9–11. In this passage, Jesus admonishes us to have a more accurate picture of the Father, as one who generously gives good gifts to his children. "You parents—if your children ask for a loaf of bread, do you give them a stone instead? Or if they ask for a fish, do you give them a snake? So if you sinful people know how to give good gifts to your children, how much more will your heavenly Father give good gifts to those who ask him."

What is your perception of God today? Is he the Father who loves you? Is he generous? Does he lavish gifts upon you? Or do you see the world as a place of scarcity, in which you have to compete for favor and attention, seeking to supply your own needs?

SELF: ORPHAN OR SON?

What do you see when you look in the mirror?

A favored child or an abandoned orphan?

Without knowing it, it's easy for us to get caught up in the orphan mindset. The following lists contrast the self-perception of an orphan with the self-perception of a beloved child:

ORPHAN vs. SON/DAUGHTER

UNWANTED	CHERISHED
FORGOTTEN	~~REMEMBERED~~
LEFT BEHIND	~~PURSUED~~
ALONE	PART of a FAMILY
PRESERVATION	ABUNDANCE
CYNICAL	TRUSTING

My parents divorced when I was in high school. Mom was out drinking. Dad was with his new girlfriend. And though I was in the house with my siblings, we were all alone. We felt overwhelmed by a sense of abandonment, softly crying in our separate quarters. Soon afterward, our beautifully kept house became embarrassingly unkempt. Our outdoor pool turned into a swamp. It was a vivid picture of what was happening in our lives and in our hearts. Living with abandonment left me hard-hearted. I responded by living like an orphaned child. I was reckless, experimenting with crazy compulsions. I lived like I had no one really caring for me. I acted out of anger, a sense of injustice, like I'd been ripped off.

Eventually, at a youth retreat in the Rocky Mountains, I sensed God speaking to me. That day, out of the millions of people in the world, God saw me. He heard my cry, and I heard him call my name. I felt overwhelmed by his presence. I soaked in the Father's love. From that moment, I knew that God had a destiny for me. I read the Bible as if it were a personal letter written by a father to his favored son. I embraced the truth that God is a Father to the fatherless. Every earthly father will fall short and fail us in some way. Wherever our earthly fathers are in terms of their ability to love us, God will fill the gaps our fathers can't satisfy.

Do you see yourself as God sees you?

OTHERS: BEAUTIFULLY FLAWED

I can still remember Leighton Ford looking at me as we were wrapping up a three-year leadership program. This was at a time in my life when I was looking for a father figure to guide me. I had prayed for a mentor. God provided Leighton. We were in North Carolina that day to celebrate our graduation from the program with other leaders from around the country. Leighton walked up to me. He laid his hands on my shoulders.

"David," he said, "God is going to use you. You will impact people from all around the world." These were probably not his exact words, but this is what I heard as he looked into my eyes.

As he spoke to me, I knew I was hearing God speaking through him. To this day, I can still remember his hands on my shoulders. They were the hands of blessing. His blessing has left an imprint on my life. He saw me.

How we see others affects the way we live. If we are able to see others only as critics, we are doomed to a life of people pleasing. If we are able to see others only as objects to be used, we will never know relational intimacy.

People are beautifully flawed. We all have the potential for greatness. Each person has a natural proclivity toward evil and destructive behavior. Our perceptions of others must be balanced by the truth, because the way we see others impacts the way we live, think, and act. While man focuses on outward appearances, XEALOTS are in solidarity with a God who looks at the heart.

Leighton saw my potential. He saw a divine seed planted in me. My shame-filled view of myself turned into a vision of limitless possibilities.

WORK: THE WAY OF CHUANG TZU

I first encountered a poem titled "The Woodcarver" in the book *The Way of Chuang Tzu* by the late Trappist monk Thomas Merton. The poem is still relevant today.

The Woodcarver

Khing, the master carver, made a bell stand
Of precious wood. When it was finished,
All who saw it were astounded. They said it must be
The work of spirits.
The Prince of Lu said to the master carver:
"What is your secret?"

Khing replied: "I am only a workman:
I have no secret. There is only this:
When I began to think about the work you commanded
I guarded my spirit, did not expend it
On trifles, that were not to the point.
I fasted in order to set
My heart at rest.

After three days fasting,
I had forgotten gain and success.
After five days
I had forgotten praise or criticism.
After seven days
I had forgotten my body
With all its limbs.

"By this time all thought of your Highness
And of the court had faded away.
All that might distract me from the work
Had vanished.
I was collected in the single thought
Of the bell stand.

"Then I went to the forest
To see the trees in their own natural state.
When the right tree appeared before my eyes,
The bell stand also appeared in it, clearly, beyond doubt.
All I had to do was to put forth my hand
And begin.

"If I had not met this particular tree
There would have been
No bell stand at all.

"What happened?
My own collected thought
Encountered the hidden potential in the wood;
From this live encounter came the work
Which you ascribe to the spirits."[2]

This poem speaks to our perception of work. It draws our
attention to the relationship between what we believe and what

we do. In the poem, the master carver, Khing, is praised for his work of art. Even the Prince of Lu takes notice and subtly escalates the level of praise when he asks, "What is your secret?" The adoring crowd wants to know how the woodcarver was able to craft such an amazing bell stand from a piece of wood.

But notice the way the carver replies: "I am only a workman." The woodcarver has a clear perception of himself and his abilities. He sees himself as a simple workman, a servant. His humility and his honest assessment of himself keep him from distracting visions of greatness. In the midst of receiving praise from others, he is able to maintain personal clarity and focus.

We spend much of our time focused on what we consider to be the ideal type of work. But what if our occupation is less about what we want and more about what we're being asked to do? What if our work is more of a calling? This calling emerges out of a context of close family friendship. In fact, the greatest vision comes out of great relationships. This calling is not simply about a job description. This is about understanding our essence to fulfill our destiny. Remember that when God revealed his plans to Moses, to free the thousands from slavery in Egypt, Moses responded by asking God, "Who am I?"[3] And God said to him, "You're with me." That was all that mattered. It wasn't the specific tasks that God was asking Moses to do that mattered most of all (though those were important). What was most important was that Moses grasped that he was *with* God, *in* God. That he was part of the family. Whatever would come, God had his back.

Our job description is equally simple. Be with the Father. Follow his lead. What matters most is not the specific job we do; it's whether we are following Jesus and doing the Father's will. All of our work is sacred work. The excellence of all our work speaks to who he is. And the extraordinary spirit of our work emerges any place we serve. This is the creative, life-giving force supernaturally in us. This extraordinary spirit is evident in the lives of Daniel, Shadrach, Meshach, and Abednego. They were followers of God in the context of a secular kingdom. However, their lives stood out because of the excellence of their work and their extraordinary spirit.

Notice, also, that in the poem, this ordinary woodcarver has reached a place in his life and work where he has learned to forget gain and success, praise and criticism. He has even lost a sense of his own body, his own presence in the work. His work is no longer about him; it's about the simple joy of creating something. This new focus allows him to truly see, to envision the potential of the wood. As he lays aside what other people want from his work, a sense of freedom flows out of his heart and his mind. The work of his ordinary hands leads to an extraordinary masterpiece.

Notice, finally, that there is a work of preparation for the woodcarver. He spends time in fasting as a way of envisioning the result of his work, training his mind and his thoughts to forget worldly gain and success. Fasting, the denial of food for the body, is about holding our appetite at bay. Because food is so essential, the discipline of fasting affects us spiritually and emotionally. It helps to deconstruct our false self: the titles, academic degrees, ancestral pedigree, accomplishments, possessions, and relationships that so easily shape our identity in ways that are fragmented and false.

FORTY DAYS

I once had the opportunity to participate in a forty-day fast. Honestly, I felt like I was dying! I'd gaze at people talking to me.

Their lips would remind me of two hamburger patties coming together. (I'm sure I was delusional!) Fasting is such a powerful practice because it reminds us of the call of Jesus to die to ourselves, to our egos. We experience this death by dying to our primal desire for food. The hunger never goes away, but we learn to replace our desire for food with spiritual food. St. Benedict, a sixth-century monk, once said, "Daily keep your death before your eyes." You're not ready to live until you're willing to die.

Spiritual disciplines like fasting, solitude, and meditation create a space in our hearts, a place of inner preparation. These movements help to transform us from idealists to realists. We are called to be hopeful realists who see and recognize the truth about God, ourselves, others, and work. In this inner space we create through the disciplines, we mystically connect more deeply with God and with others.

In addition to fasting from food, it can be helpful to fast from the things we depend on spiritually and emotionally. My daughter, along with some of her friends, did a three-day "makeup and mirrors" fast. Why? They told me that they felt their generation is too consumed with image. They chose this type of a fast to remind themselves that they aren't dependent on the opinions of others for identity or security. After their image fast, the girls said their perspective and focus changed as they looked at others. They began to see Jesus in the people around them as they stopped comtemplating their own image.

Or have you ever considered fasting from various technological devices, letting go of your dependence on cell phones, recorded music, movies, and computers for a period of time? Eliminating our use of digital technology can also be a way of creating inner space, enabling the Spirit of God to shape us and speak to us apart from the hum of our devices.

When I travel through some of the larger cities throughout the world, I cannot help but notice that people behave like zombies. Their dull expressions and glazed looks are illuminated by the glowing screens of their digital devices. People walk by one another without paying any attention to the people near them. They stare and type into their little machines. And if they aren't poking at smartphones, they're nodding their heads to the beat of their MP3 players.

I wonder if fasting from our use of certain forms of technology would cause us to see people in new ways. I wonder if we'd notice things we had never seen before. Would we remember ideas we had forgotten? Perhaps there are new dreams waiting to come alive, or new songs waiting to be written. Are songs unreleased inside our hearts because of the distraction of digital technology? We are so mesmerized by the things we have created that we miss out on the most dynamic creation of all — human beings made in the image of their Creator! In the midst of so much noise, we are missing out on the One who is often heard in moments of silence and in quiet whispers. The art of understanding nuance and subtle hues requires a slower pace and watchfulness. We have to pay attention.

There is no shortcut to seeing our work in the way of the woodcarver. I wish it were a simple discipline. The truth is that most of us will walk down this road of self-denial only when tragedy forces us to. In such moments, God invites us to see ourselves. He desires us to know him as our God and Father. In these moments of pain, we die to ourselves and cultivate a brokenness that leads us to seek God. When the noises fade and the quiet reemerges, the silence becomes a channel for the voice of God to speak to us. Our inner hunger gives way to fullness. Our thirst is quenched.

FADING ILLUSIONS

Are you living with integrity? Your life, your image, the face you put on every day—is it all an illusion? Where does the facade end and the truth begin? That's a question we all answer differently. Once again, fasting and time spent in solitude will illuminate truth.

One of the greatest illusions I have is my ability to control things and people. I've bought into the lie that says, "Yes, I'm in full control of my life." I used to feel a bit like the character Chuck Noland, whom Tom Hanks plays in the movie *Castaway*. A FedEx executive, Noland wrongly assumes that he can control everything that happens in his life, right down to the second. Even after learning that his friend's wife has been diagnosed with cancer, he still thinks, "We'll beat it." Nothing can shatter his illusion of control. And then, his plane crashes. He finds himself stranded, alone on an island for several years. And his time on the island becomes a season of fasting for him. While he is there, alone and struggling to survive, he finds he can control nothing. At one point, in a fit of despair, he tries to kill himself and fails. "I couldn't even control how I was going to die," he realizes.

This scene reminds me of a poignant moment when my wife, Rebecca, and I were talking about the challenge of having a disease like cancer. She commented that people often turn to God and ask, "Why me, God?" She then concluded, "That's the wrong question, Dave. We should be saying, 'Why *not* me?'"

Our lives are not really ours to control. They are gifts we receive with gratitude.

Take time regularly to fast and listen to God. Find a place to meet him and receive the guidance you need. Soak in the truth. Let him sweep away the lies. Let him expose the illusions in your heart. Make way for a live encounter with the truth, the person of Jesus. Make space in your life for conversations with him. Give him full access to your life. Let him guide and illuminate your path. It is in the presence of his light that we vividly see what's real. The illusions we carry burn away in the fire of his love for us.[4] Perhaps what the world needs from us is not simply another proclamation of truth but rather for us to be the truth.

3

SUCCESS

mission zero

If you try to hang on to your life, you will lose it. But if you give up your life for my sake and for the sake of the Good News, you will save it.

— MARK 8:35

IF YOU could draw a picture of success, what would it look like?

Now, suppose you were trying to depict the idea of success on a graph. What would it look like? Where would you start? How would you draw your path to success?

Perhaps your drawing is different from mine. Most of us would probably envision success to look like the graph on page 46.

This is what we're taught to strive for: the "up-and-to-the-right" life. An up-and-to-the-right house filled with up-and-to-the-right kids who all go to up-and-to-the-right schools. Success is defined as bigger and more. We want more space, larger cars, and super-sized products. We're thirsty for the extra large. For most of us, more is the definition of success.

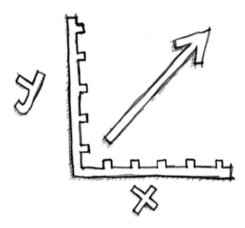

A couple I know who lived in Bangkok, Jeff and Tara Russell, prepared a Christmas letter to their family and friends. This letter included an exciting announcement: "We're moving to California!" From their perspective and that of their friends and family, this was a positive move. It was a move in the direction of success, an up-and-to-the-right change in their lives.

But a strange thing happened to them. Immediately after they put the letter in the mail, they realized that the decision to move to California was a mistake. Suddenly, it didn't seem like the right thing to do. Instead, they decided to stay in Thailand for at least another year. Since they had already mailed out the first letter, Tara sent out a second to their friends and family members — a New Year's letter. Those who knew them were surprised to hear of the change in their plans.

Just after they sent out that second letter, they realized that they had to type up yet another one. There was another unexpected change in their plans.

Not again, they thought.

Yes. Again.

So Tara sent out the third letter. Now, if you were to graph their dreams of success over the course of this week, I think their graph would probably look something like this:

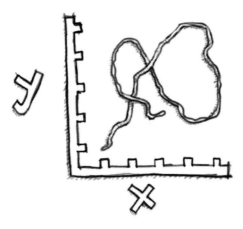

You can probably imagine the embarrassment Tara felt as she sent out that third letter. But the truth is, we never know when our lives will change like this. We need to prepare ourselves

Tara and Jeff Russell

for the unexpected. Success is rarely a straight line. In God's economy, success looks more like the path of a confused ant!

YOU KNOW WHAT THEY SAY

Bigger.

Better.

Faster.

Stronger.

More growth.

More bling.

More space.

Build your own brand.

At every stage of life, we scale up. Every time our income increases, we raise our standard of living right along with it, guaranteeing that the pursuit of success will never end. We never quite reach the carrot that the world dangles in front of us. There is always more to be pursued. So why do we chase after it all, if we know that it never ends?

Our consumeristic, materially driven culture conditions us to respond with intense addictive behavior. We all show signs of the nervous energy of someone needing another fix to get them to the "next level." Add the pressures of family, job, and everyday life; it's no wonder we feel the constant pressure to "make it." To be someone. Our parents, our spouses — the very people who love us and live in our homes — use the metrics of worldly success to measure us and score our lives.

I think this is especially true of immigrant families in the United States, where it is common for parents to regularly remind their children how much they sacrificed to be where they are today. Children in these families are raised with high expectations to achieve success. Some families, so consumed with this dream of monetary success for their children, even give their kids names reflecting their greatest hope in life. They name their son Harvard or their daughter Mercedes.

I wish I were joking.

If you look around long enough, you'll notice that many people — especially those who follow Christ — live with a constant sense of internal conflict. Our definitions of success are rooted deeply in our culture, the values our parents taught us, and the concerns of our peers and friends. Success never satisfies. We continue to ask, What does it really mean to be successful? And why is it that so many people who seem to achieve success, the up-and-to-the-right life, feel so dissatisfied?

Our quest for worldly success leaves us aching for more. We experience an internal gnawing ache of emptiness. We hunger for something that will fill the void of our fractured identity. We settle for substitutes that might taste good but are spiritually unhealthy. We crave real food, yet we settle for cotton candy. Strict diets are necessary for healthy living. Here are a few dieting tips that might prove helpful as you encounter the fast food of the world.

DOWNSIZE

The subprime mortgage crisis and the resulting crash of the banking world in 2007 reminded us that we're never too big to fail. Just because a company has higher profits this year over last doesn't mean it is successful. Success is about more than profits or size. It's all too easy to increase numbers and profit margins using unethical and dehumanizing methods. In his gospel, Mark reminds us that success, in God's economy, carries a cost: "If you try to hang on to your life, you will lose it. But if you give up your life for my sake and for the sake of the Good News, you will save it. And what do you benefit if you gain the whole world but lose your own soul? Is anything worth more than your soul?"[1] There are paths to success that will earn you applause and money but ultimately rob you of life itself.

THREE HUNDRED

You may recall the story of Gideon in the book of Judges. Gideon, ready to battle his enemies, was told by God to decrease his numbers. God downsized his forces from an army of thousands to a mere three hundred fighting men.[2] Three hundred men faced off against several thousand mighty warriors who were ready to eat them for lunch.

Or consider King David. David commanded armies, but he placed his life in the hands of thirty valiant special operatives, his mighty men.[3] Even Jesus, who changed the world through his teachings and his sacrificial death on the cross, chose to focus his attention on a small core of twelve below-average blue-collar misfits. Instead of commanding empires, establishing programs, and starting services for the thousands of people in need, Jesus focused on this small group, teaching them and training them to carry on the mission. In God's economy, the small movements of the kingdom consume the empires of their day. God has a pattern of using small and seemingly inconsequential things — like a tiny mustard seed, which grows into a tree for birds to rest on, or a handful of loaves and fish, which are multiplied to feed thousands — to effect lasting change. Big isn't necessarily bad, but when we see things through God's eyes, it can seem a bit overrated. We are called to engage the world. We don't need masses. Yet we can't do it alone.

BIGGER IS NOT BETTER

Jesus spent most of his three-year ministry healing and teaching. And when he taught, his teaching was most often about the kingdom of God: "God's Dream Society on Earth."[4] The kingdom was constantly on Jesus' mind. He discussed it with his closest followers and regularly taught parables about the kingdom to the crowds that gathered to hear him. Yet when Jesus spoke of the kingdom, he wasn't interested in making it seem larger than life. He compared it to a mustard seed, the tiniest of seeds. He taught that the kingdom is like yeast in a loaf of bread. Not very impressive pictures.

We tend to overvalue things that are large and undervalue things that are small and seemingly of little consequence. The power of what God wants to accomplish tends to get diffused when we think big. Because of our limited vision and resources, we typically look for one-size-fits-all processes when we are trying to make a difference. But this ignores the benefits of a customized approach to human development. The reality is that it takes only a few to provoke significant change. And the ones who cause the greatest change are often the ones living on the fringe — the creatives and the entrepreneurs. They can be rich or poor, educated or uneducated, part of the elite or members of the lowest caste. It doesn't matter. They are the ones the masses will follow.

The second problem with focusing on the big solution is that it is often heavy on financial resources and human capital. Resources are quickly exhausted for the sake of maintaining the large structures we create. People often forget that God has already equipped us to do what he asks us to do. The resources are probably already in our hands.

NAVY SEAL TEAM SIX

I worked with a special forces operative once. He shared with me that the most elite fighting force in the world is Navy Seal Team Six. If the president is kidnapped, Navy Seal Team Six is called in. How many men do they have? Only about three hundred. They have, though, a support team of more than fourteen hundred. The size of their budget? He said it's the size of the marines' budget!

Sometimes small is better. Small can be adaptive, flexible, focused, and potent.

THE MARGINS CREATE MOVEMENTS

The apostle Paul gives us a clear breakdown of responsibilities and roles in 1 Corinthians 3 when he describes how the process of growth occurs in relationship to the Father: "After all, who is Apollos? Who is Paul? We are only God's servants through whom you believed the Good News. Each of us did the work the Lord gave us. I planted the seed in your hearts, and Apollos watered it, but it was God who made it grow. It's not important who does the planting, or who does the watering. What's important is that God makes the seed grow. The one who plants and the one who waters work together with the same purpose. And both will be rewarded for their own hard work. For we are both God's workers. And you are God's field. You are God's building."[5]

Our role in God's economy is clear. We plant and water the seeds. But Scripture tells us that it's God's responsibility to cause the growth.

UNSPECTACULAR SUCCESS

I remember the work of my mother and father, who put in fifty- to sixty-hour weeks without fanfare or praise. They simply wanted to give their kids the best life they could. They sacrificed themselves so that we could live a better life.

Success in God's economy frequently begins with the unspectacular. It may be hidden behind modest numbers. It often appears to be small and inconsequential, but that's precisely where God unveils his love, grace, and power. God loves to demonstrate his strength through those whom the world considers weak, his wisdom through those considered to be fools.[6] Some of the greatest works in God's kingdom are often hidden and unseen: the habitual prayers of a grandfather for his grandchildren, a mother sacrificing her sleep to nurse at 2:00 a.m., a caregiver comforting an elderly person in a nursing home, aid workers digging wells in the hot sun, a father working three jobs in manufacturing plants to support his family. This is the work that happens in the common, everyday places; our homes and workplaces become laboratories for the kingdom, where no one sees the fruit that is produced but God himself. It is in the midst of the mundane that life is born.

MEASURING SUCCESS

Business gurus will tell you that you are the one who "makes it happen." You are the catalyst for your own success. Your decisions and expectations largely determine whether you succeed in life. It comes down to your initiative, your ability to generate momentum.

Really?

God teaches us that success is more than self-generated energy; it's about the way we get there, the journey. Success, in God's kingdom, is about living more of a responsive life than a life of self-driven initiative. Ultimately, how success is defined in your life depends on your unique, God-given destiny. Success is met by following the Father, down whatever road he leads. It may be an expedition or it may be uneventfully short. It can be pleasurable or it can be painful, filled with trials and challenges.

Sometimes we end up walking the road alone, while other times we journey with others.

Jesus had a very clear purpose for his life, a purpose that clarified how to define success. He described it this way: "For even the Son of Man came not to be served but to serve others and to give his life as a ransom for many."[7] Jesus believed that the primary pursuit of his life was to radically give of himself for the sake of others. For many of us, our primary hope is to have our needs met and to fulfill our ambitions and dreams. But Jesus was clear about his purpose: sacrificing his life as a ransom so others could live.

We get tunnel vision when we relentlessly focus on finding the ideal job. But of far greater value to our lives is hearing and responding to our calling. Our occupation isn't the key to success. It's knowing our vocation, our calling—to live as a servant, like Jesus. Our first calling is to follow the Father wherever he may lead, to become a radical giver. We can be successful anywhere doing anything, if we follow the Father and serve.

God gave us a clear mission, and it's the same mission. We are called to love God with all our being and then to love others, especially those who are abnormal to us. Our success in living out this mission is measured in small acts, unseen movements, things that we do or say that are unappreciated. These movements are a response to God's initiative in and around us.

The life of a XEALOT is a life of response, a life of following God rather than always trying to make things happen.

Give me a team of people who know how to watch, wait, listen, people who fast, pray, and surrender rather than always trying to take control. These are the ones developing sensitivity to the Holy Spirit; they understand how to let God guide them through life.

That's what Jesus was talking about when he told Peter, "When you were young, you were able to do as you liked; you dressed yourself and went wherever you wanted to go. But when you are old, you will stretch out your hands, and others will dress you and take you where you don't want to go."[8] He's describing spiritual maturity in a way that's opposite to how we normally see it. Normally, we think that when we're young, we have to do what other people tell us. Our parents put us in car seats and drive us around; our teachers give us assignments and grade us on how closely we meet their expectations. We look forward to the time when we can get our driver's license, drive wherever we want to go, and do whatever we want to do. Growing up equates to more independence.

But Jesus suggests that kind of independence is a sign of immaturity. It's when you're young that you go wherever you want to go. When you're old, he says, you "stretch out your hands" and allow yourself to be led. For Jesus, true maturity equates to more dependence on the Holy Spirit.

It's funny — you almost have to read that paragraph a couple of times to get it right. It feels like there's a typo. But no, that's the XEALOT life — not making things happen but letting things happen, flowing with God without having to force it.

Waiting, being still, and being silent demonstrates you're letting God lead. You trust him.

It makes me think of baseball. Some people think that baseball is the most boring sport. They watch for hours and think, "Nothing is happening."

What makes baseball amazing is not what happens but what's about to happen. Every pitch is rich with possibility. It could result in a home run or the start of a rally or an out that changes the course of the game.

That's how waiting on God feels. Even when it's over a long period of time, it's not boring; it's exciting. You have a constant sense of expectation.

Attempting to make things happen is like the drunk fan running onto the field, thinking his "initiative" is adding something to the game.

But sober fans wait, hearts pounding, feeling something they may not be able to put into words, something that may not be well-defined. In the unknown, they hope.

When we measure success by the size of our influence or the numbers in our bank accounts, we miss out on some of the most significant moves of God. Jesus is the perfect example of this. By normal human standards of success, Jesus was a failure. His story begins where most stories end, at the pinnacle of success. After all, he was (and is) the eternal Son of God, the King of All Kings, and the Lord of All Lords. He possesses all the attributes of deity: omnipotence, omniscience, and omnipresence. Yet, as we read in Philippians 2:6–7, he chose a path of declension: "Being in very nature God, [he] did not consider equality with God something to be used to his own advantage; rather, he made himself nothing by taking the very nature of a servant, being made in human likeness" (NIV). The Son of God left his position in heaven not to be served but to serve. And not only did he come to serve but he chose to serve in the most unlikely of ways. He was born in a "small" place, raised in the marginalized, blue-collar town of Nazareth. People often remarked of his hometown, "Can anything good come from Nazareth?" It was the last place you'd look for a king.

Though he was the wisest man who ever lived, Jesus worked with his hands as a common laborer for much of his adult life. When he started his official teaching ministry, the guys he chose to roll with were a crew of misfits. Few would have made it through the first round of job applications at most companies today. They did nothing to enhance his status or reputation.

Perhaps the greatest scandal of all, though, was that this man — God incarnate — eventually was brutally beaten, whipped, spat upon, and crucified on a Roman cross. By common standards of success, by the judgment of worldly wisdom, it made no sense. Why would the King of All Kings agree to be executed alongside common criminals? Why would the very definition of success agree to endure such shame? Why would he humbly refuse to retaliate? Why did he choose love over the flexing of military muscle. The way of Jesus was the *Via Dolorosa*, the Way of Suffering. It was a literal dying to self.

This is not a path any of us would willingly choose. What parent would consider this a successful life for their child? No, this graph is our worst nightmare: starting out in the upper right and heading sharply down and to the left, a graph depicting failure, disappointment, and pain.

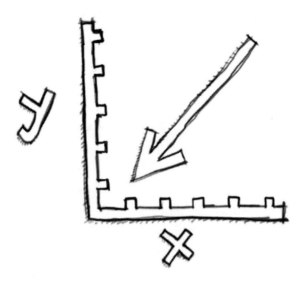

But here is what really matters: regardless of how the world might rate Jesus' life, his Father was pleased. That is the true measure of success. It doesn't matter what the opinion polls said, who Jesus chose to align himself with, or how many disciples he produced in his lifetime. The success of his life was measured by his obedience more than even by his passion.

I once heard the story of a young piano player. He had just finished playing a concert. He walked off the stage to a standing ovation. Backstage, his manager urged him to go back out for an encore. The young man refused.

"Come on, they all love you!" the manager said.

"No, not everyone," said the young man. "Did you see that old man in the back? He's not standing."

"What's the big deal? He's one guy out of an entire crowd."

"No," the pianist replied. "That old man is my teacher."

"And what do you benefit if you gain the whole world but lose your own soul?"[9] For all the energy we expend seeking success, what matters most is knowing how our lives will be judged.

Because in the end, success has nothing to do with pleasing the masses. It's about obeying the One.

MISSION ZERO

Every year, you can find magazines, blogs, and books telling us which companies are the largest, as measured by the numbers of their people or the size of their profits. Or you can read about the one hundred fastest-growing organizations or businesses. Most of these lists assume that size equals influence. The larger one is the more influential. But are the largest organizations making the most difference in their communities and in the world? If we don't use size to determine success, what metric should we use instead? If success isn't determined by quantity, what do we use to measure success? Maybe there's an additional metric we can observe.

Perhaps the only number that really matters is zero.

What if we worked to have zero orphans in our cities?

Zero foster children? Zero abused children?

What if we labored so that there were zero homeless in our community?

Zero divorces? Zero human-trafficking victims?

Rather than attracting the masses to our carefully planned agenda, what if we sought to eliminate the problems that plague our world?

Could zero be the new metric for success?

Something happens to leaders when they become fixated on the masses. Mass-movement thinking clouds our minds and diffuses the ground-level impact of our strategies. "Thinking big" can actually lessen the impact we might have had. A primary focus on the big can actually diffuse the potency of both the individual and the organization. The programs that tend to be created for the masses are unattractive to margins composed of the creative and the challenged. Why is this? Quite simply, most of us lack the capacity to think on a larger scale. Our attempts at getting bigger lead to one-size-fits-all initiatives. We create programs that move people through systems but lack the customized touch that true human development requires. We might have "graduates" of our programs and fill quotas, while our students lack adequate preparation for the real world. We need to seriously ask ourselves whether we are being pulled by the gravity of our culture's assumptions about success.

To be fair, the Bible isn't necessarily opposed to large numbers. We find them throughout Scripture. Consider the three thousand people who came to know God on Pentecost, and the multitude of five thousand men (and more women and children) that came to listen to Jesus teach. The fact that masses are attracted to something or that people respond in large numbers doesn't mean it's wrong. But large numbers can be misleading. We forget that large movements of people don't start out that way. They start small. The mass conversion of three thousand people at Pentecost began with a small band of disciples waiting upon the Lord for several weeks in prayer. This small group was willing to give what they had to offer. The Holy Spirit empowered them. These were unlearned men — fools in the eyes of the world — but God used them to stir the hearts of thousands. The feeding of the five thousand, that massive crowd that came to hear Jesus teach, started with a small boy, five loaves of bread, and two fish. Following the Father may lead to larger numbers, but you don't get there by focusing on quantity. You arrive at success by allowing God to work through your weakness. It's about allowing his power to be expressed through the foolishness of a contrarian life. God's way of measuring success validates those who feel small and unnoticed. He loves those working on the fringe, in the places that others avoid. While it's popular to focus on large urban centers, God will gravitate to the margins of a city or to the rural villages of a country.

Whose definition of success are you seeking? Consider the words of the apostle Paul to the Corinthian church. This was a church that had become enamored with worldly wisdom. She forgot the countercultural message of the cross, the way of suffering and self-sacrifice:

> The message of the cross is foolish to those who are headed for destruction! But we who are being saved know it is the very power of God. As the Scriptures say, "I will destroy the wisdom of the wise and discard the intelligence of the intelligent."
>
> So where does this leave the philosophers, the scholars, and the world's brilliant debaters? God has made the wisdom of this world look foolish. Since God in his wisdom saw to it that the world would never know him through human wisdom, he has used our foolish preaching to save those who believe. It is foolish to the Jews, who ask for signs from heaven. And it is foolish to the Greeks, who seek human wisdom. So when we preach that Christ was crucified, the Jews are offended and the Gentiles say it's all nonsense.
>
> But to those called by God to salvation, both Jews and Gentiles, Christ is the power of God and the wisdom of God. This foolish plan of God is wiser than the wisest of human plans, and God's weakness is stronger than the greatest of human strength.
>
> Remember, dear brothers and sisters, that few of you were wise in the world's eyes or powerful or wealthy when

God called you. Instead, God chose things the world considers foolish in order to shame those who think they are wise. And he chose things that are powerless to shame those who are powerful. God chose things despised by the world, things counted as nothing at all, and used them to bring to nothing what the world considers important. As a result, no one can ever boast in the presence of God.

God has united you with Christ Jesus. For our benefit God made him to be wisdom itself. Christ made us right with God; he made us pure and holy, and he freed us from sin. Therefore, as the Scriptures say, "If you want to boast, boast only about the LORD."[10]

God chooses the things and the people that the world considers foolish. Why? To shame the wise. He chooses the powerless to shame the powerful. Why? So that none of us can boast that our success is our own.

It's not an easy road. It may seem pointless at times. But God uses us—in our insignificance and weakness—to accomplish his purposes. Perhaps that's why the apostle Paul could say, "I take pleasure in my weaknesses."[11] God's strength is actually perfected in our weakness. Experiencing God's grace in the places where we struggle fuels a radical, zealous love. After a prostitute finished washing Jesus' feet with her hair and her tears (a taboo act), Jesus looked at those around him who were silently judging the woman and said to them, "The one who has been forgiven much, loves much." The more we understand our need for grace, the more we are free to love with recklessness.

I close this chapter with a note from Tara Russell, a woman I consider a modern-day Joan of Arc. She and her husband are the couple I mentioned at the start of this chapter, whose lives we graphed. She writes,

> Thank you for what you wrote in this chapter and shared. I dream of a zero world, a zero kingdom, and I'm continually blown away by God's approach to getting there, but trying to trust him and walk in faith. Boldly.
>
> Of course you can use our story; it's a bizarre testimony of God directing our unlikely paths toward his perfect plans and not ours.
>
> Being an engineer, I of course appreciate the graphs, and you got very close in the graph of our life! It just has a lot more downward, chaotic scribbles included now (but feels very upward in joy—true riches—living in our sweet spot).
>
> We have so much more than we need *and* get to do work we were created carefully for; it's so humbling.

Today, the Russell family resides in Boise, Idaho, working with refugees, among other initiatives.[12] Their lives are far from stale.

Our lives can feel chaotic, yet we are moving upward in joy.

4

SCARS

the embrace of pain

In my deepest wound, I see your glory and it dazzles me.

— St. Augustine

I WAS in my room, alone. Crying. I could faintly hear the sobs of my brother and my sister down the hall in their rooms.

Our hearts were torn.

Our future was uncertain.

Our family was broken.

I remember thinking, "Will this nightmare ever end?"

My mother's past remains a mystery to me. Though she occasionally shared stories of her life growing up as a child in Korea, there were still moments when I felt as if I knew nothing about her. She would talk, briefly, about the bombing raids of the Korean War, of running through the streets as people were diving for cover around her. Her primary contribution to the family, as a child, was the responsibility of gathering water. She had to walk long distances. From her youngest days, my mother

had known nothing but a life of hard work. My struggles as a young person growing up in America paled in comparison.

My mother married young, first to a Korean soldier who abused her. Their short-lived marriage ended when she fled, taking my older sister with her. Soon, my mother met a young, handsome American soldier with blue eyes and wavy hazel-brown locks. He swept her off her feet. She married again. A year into this second marriage, I was born—in a military hospital in Seoul, Korea. Eventually, my mother and father traveled to the United States to pursue the American dream: education for their children, a nice house, a boat, cars, a swimming pool, and all the things that meant worldly success. Because they worked hard, they achieved many of their dreams. Our family was the envy of many. My friends would come over to party. Our house was like the neighborhood Disneyland. They would tell me how cool our family was. They wished they had parents just like mine. Everyone thought we were the perfect American family, the family that had it all, the family that had it all together.

I thought they were right about the Gibbons family. I never saw my parents fight. They hardly disagreed. That is, until one unforgettable evening, when all hell broke loose.

Our family began to unravel when my mom locked herself into my father's Chevy truck, one she bought for him as a gift. Since my father loved new vehicles, she tried every few years to get him a new vehicle to drive. So one night, in a fit of despair and frustration, my mom went to his truck because it represented everything she had given to him—the marriage, the sacrifice. She found sanctuary in that place. It was a place to vent her emotions and say how she really felt.

How it all seemed so worthless.

Her marriage. Her love. Her sacrifice.

She sobbed inside the truck, a mixture of anger, disbelief, and anguish etched on her face. Then, she began slashing the seats of that Chevy truck with a kitchen knife. My dad wasn't sure what to do, so he called the police, hoping they could intervene. Three police cars responded. They parked in front of our house. Our neighbors were shocked—even bewildered—as they looked out their windows at the assortment of police cars in front of the Gibbons' home.

I later learned the cause of my mother's behavior. She had discovered, that very night, that my dad was seeing someone else.

Because she had been abused in her first marriage, the news of his betrayal provoked her worst fears. Suddenly, her childhood pain, with all of its terrors, returned. My mom felt she was alone again. She faced the trauma of losing everything she had dreamed of. It had all been embodied in my father, in her marriage. She had given everything to him, and now she feared losing it all. She also felt a deeply rooted cultural sense of shame overwhelming her. The shame threatened to destroy not only her life but the future she had worked to achieve for her children. She was betrayed.

Though the police officers were able to talk her out of the truck, my mother never fully recovered from that awful evening. She soon fell into a deep depression. Alcohol became her drug. She began staying out later into the evening. Suffering from multiple ulcers and constant anxiety, she became erratic in her eating habits. Mom dramatically lost weight. Her life was falling apart.

I still remember the day, several years later, when my parents divorced. I sat in the sterile courtroom that day watching the dissolution of my family, the end of a long and destructive process that began many years earlier. To one side of the judge sat my mom, and on the other side sat my dad. Throughout the proceedings that day, my mother looked over at my father. Several times, she pleaded with him to come back, to keep our family together. But my dad remained unfazed.

It was over.

My mother's pain became our pain. It shaped our lives. In the beginning, it felt like a scar I wanted to cover and hide. That scar reminds me of chronic emotional pain. Scars are reference points, ways of connecting us to the hurt, the tragedy, and that feeling of being alone. While the intensity of emotion isn't with me any longer, the scar still remains.

After my parents' divorce, I went down a destructive path.

While it was easy to blame my parents for the choices I made, blaming them was also an excuse to live a wild life. There was no one around to keep me accountable or to instruct me in the right way to live. My siblings and I suffered the guilt of association. As children, we felt the weight of being from a family with divorced parents, a reality that was not as common then as it is today. Whenever we went on dates, the questions inevitably came up. Our dates' parents harbored doubts about our potential for long-term commitment and loyalty in marriage. Not only were we a racially mixed family (which was not popular at that time), now we were also a broken family.

I found myself trying to numb my pain through alcohol, drugs, and football. I found that playing football was a socially acceptable way for me to unleash my anger. In fact, I soon learned that my coaches would reward me for this! Some may have wondered what was fueling my rage, but they never asked. I made the first string and started feeling good again after seeing some success as a player. But soon, even this became an area of disappointment and frustration for me. My dad never came to watch me play. I hoped to see him there, proud of me.

He didn't even show up to see me graduate.

When you feel like a misfit and you begin to think that all is lost, it's easy to wonder, "God, why me? Why did my parents get divorced? When is this bad dream going to end? What's the purpose behind it all?" I often thought, "If there really is a God, I can't believe that he would let us suffer through such dark nights."

I know that pain is a bitter pill to swallow. We don't want it. We pray that God will give us a pass this time. We hope he will provide a detour around this obstacle. Many of us are experts in pain avoidance, and for good reason! Who wants to feel the sting of failure or the overwhelming hurt of brokenness in our relationships? We try to steer clear of difficulties. We're glad when we avoid troubles, thankful that they didn't happen to us. And when pain inevitably comes, our response is fairly predictable — we complain, run away, and get depressed. Sometimes we turn our pain outward to others and become abusive. Often, we turn inward and beat ourselves up, repeating lies that eventually become our truth and define our fragmented reality. Everything that we say and do is affected by our pain. As the saying goes, "Hurt people hurt people." And if that is our response to suffering, the cycle will never end.

But there is another way to respond. It's abnormal. The way of the XEALOT is to embrace pain and suffering as a gift. When I refer to pain, I mean our addictions, sins, weaknesses, and trials. By the way, this is one of the most important aspects of understanding your destiny. The uniqueness of the XEALOT is that he doesn't ignore or even simply confess his pain. He embraces his pain. He sees it as a gift and even as a guide. As counterintuitive as it may seem, it's in the dark seasons of life that God leads us to experience intimacy and find direction. XEALOTS recognize pain as the prelude to change, a season of new opportunities. Death leads to resurrection. Resurrection leads to ascension. Pain points us to a destiny that we could not have otherwise achieved.

It is in the struggle, dark night of brokenness that we discover the truth that God is present, even in the midst of our loss. Even the darkness is light to him.[1] Naturally, we do everything we can to avoid pain. We seek success and prosperity. We want to feel good about life, about ourselves, about our relationship with God. When life is good, it's tempting to minimize Jesus, since our need for him seems to decrease. We reduce Jesus to our good buddy, our trusted friend. For many, Jesus becomes our wishing well of good fortune. But that's not the Jesus of the Bible, the one who calls us to deny ourselves, take up our crosses, and follow him. Jesus calls us to a life of suffering.

The typical narrative that calls us to follow Jesus is focused on the end, not on the way. It's heavenly focused, but fails to address the reality of the journey. While we emphasize the resurrection power of Jesus, we cannot forget the cross. There is no shortcut. Death precedes resurrection. The path of life is open to those who first walk the path of sacrifice and suffering. Jesus calls us to follow him: "Those who love their life in this world will lose it. Those who care nothing for life in this world will keep it for eternity. Anyone who wants to be my disciple must follow me, because my servants must be where I am. And the Father will honor anyone who serves me."[2]

There are many different ways to think about what it means to live and lead out of our weakness. Living this way is the key to overcoming many sins, but it is more than a recipe for sin management. Learning to embrace our pain is a process that I describe as the "pain continuum" (see p. 72). The pain continuum helps us understand how we usually cope with our pain. The continuum of pain gives us insight that can lead to maturity and growth. While the West tends to medicate pain, the East helps us to embrace it. This, to me, is one of the most important illustrations of the book.

STAGE 1: COVERING

The initial stage of the continuum occurs when we first experience pain. Pain is the natural repercussion of dealing with our brokenness. Our immediate response to this type of

pain is to deny it. Even if we are forced to acknowledge what is happening, we seek a way of avoiding the pain. Some people never get past this stage. They live in an unhealthy state of denial. The pain only worsens. Certainly, it can be numbed at times, but it's never truly better. A person living in denial falls prey to a constant dullness of heart. He leads a disengaged life, avoiding choices and commitments that might lead to additional episodes of brokenness. Eventually life becomes a work of projecting a false self. This just adds more stress.

When we act in a way that is different from what we know is honest, we lack power in our lives. We can fool people, but our voices lack resonance. Over time, this leads us to hide who we are and cover up our weaknesses. Just like Adam and Eve in the garden of Eden, we are no longer comfortable being transparent in the light of God's truth, and we respond to our pain by hiding and covering. A dissonance rises between what we say and who we really know we are.

STAGE 2: CONFESSION

Sometimes, though, people come to a place of recognizing that something is wrong with their lives. They are able to admit that not all is right. Biblically, the act of confession is when we come to agree with God about our issues: our sins and all the ways in which we've missed the mark. When we agree with God, we take the first step toward exiting the rut of denial. Since our failure is constant, confession becomes part of the normal rhythm of those who follow Jesus. When we are honest about our pain, it's like a pressure valve is opened, releasing denial. This move toward confession is the second stage of the contrarian continuum, and it is the step that starts the healing process. Still, it's only the second stage of the journey. Most people, sadly, stop here and never experience what comes next.

The temptation for most of us is to stop growing at the moment of confession. We confess our failure. We ask God to take the pain away, hoping for instant transformation and healing. But as we struggle with our addictions, whether to alcohol or drugs, or to materialism, money, and worldly success, we must recount that we are weak and that change is rarely instantaneous. Those who belong to Alcoholics Anonymous understand that in order to stay sober, they must embrace their identity as alcoholics. Like the alcoholic in recovery, we too must embrace who we are, including our scars.

Pain at times is not a sin to confess but rather a wound to bring to light. This type of pain is from abuse or the intentional or unintentional action of someone against us. This bringing of our pain to the light allows the fresh spring winds of the Holy Spirit to heal us of deep wounds.

STAGE 3: EMBRACE

The stage of embrace is what enables a person to take responsibility for his or her sin and to see failure and healing as an integral part of the growth process. Along with our positive attributes and gifts, we also have scars that define who we are. In this stage, an individual accepts his shortcomings and the fact that he desperately needs grace.

To be clear: the movement toward embrace is not a tacit "oh well," a casual acceptance of our sins. Embracing our broken humanity is not an attempt to solve our sin problem or forever end the pain. Instead, it's about living in the tension of our ongoing brokenness and at the same time the good news of our position as children of God.

In fact, as we mature in our faith, we grow more sensitive to our weaknesses, to the things that we once ignored or paid little attention to. As we draw closer to the light, our scars are more noticeable. Perhaps this is what the apostle Paul was thinking when he described himself as the "worst of sinners" in his letter to Timothy. At the time of his writing, Paul was already an old man and had been a leader in the church for several decades. He encouraged followers of Christ to look at his own life as a model of obedience to the Lord. And yet in 1 Timothy 1:14–15 Paul writes, "The grace of our Lord was poured out on me abundantly, along with the faith and love that are in Christ Jesus. Here is a trustworthy saying that deserves full acceptance: Christ Jesus came into the world to save sinners—*of whom I am the worst*" (NIV, emphasis added). The more Paul became aware of God's goodness, the more he became aware of his own failures. Paul learned to embrace God's mercy, while recognizing the harsh truth of his own moral failures.

I also find Romans 7 to be a fascinating passage because it includes both Paul's confession of his struggle with sin and an admission of what he knows is true. Theologians have had difficulty with this passage because they find it hard to accept that Paul, a mature believer in Christ, would make such a raw admission of his ongoing, intense struggle with sin. Even after following Christ for many years and serving as a leader in the church, Paul is deeply aware of his broken humanity. I believe this was one of the reasons why he lived with such authority and power. Paul understood and managed the tension between his identity as a child of God—saved by grace—and his ongoing struggle with sin. When we don't manage this tension well, a disparity emerges in our lives. What we know is true and who we really are fail to align, and it leads to stress and drivenness as we seek to cover and hide our weaknesses.

At the conclusion of Romans 7 and continuing into chapter 8, Paul provides us with a road map for managing the tension of our ongoing struggle with pain and sin. We learn to see ourselves as simultaneously weak and strong. We learn to embrace the pain but hold onto the truth that we are sons and daughters of God, reflections of his beauty. When this happens, we live with power and authority. We become truth. The facades fade.

STAGE 4: GUIDE

As we learn to recognize our scars as gifts, they eventually become guides for our lives. Too often, we are motivated by our strengths. We run toward the things we are good at. We avoid the things we aren't good at. We attempt to ignore our more noticeable character defects. Yet as we begin to appreciate God's shaping hand in our lives, we become grateful for his molding our character through pain. In the process, we discover our true calling, the way of the cross. Our pain and weakness become the pillars that God uses as a platform, a place where we can stand and speak into the lives of others.

Nehemiah, the heroic rebuilder of the walls of Jerusalem, found his purpose through devastation. His vision grew out of his deep sorrow over the destruction of his city. God used his pain to redirect his life. Nehemiah returned to Jerusalem, a place of destruction and failure, and became the leader of the rebuilding effort. As he addressed his own pain, God illuminated his destiny.

STAGE 5: GIFT

The next stage of maturation occurs when our perspective on pain changes. In this stage, we allow the Holy Spirit to redeem our pain for the sake of the greater good. Our pain keeps us humble and dependent on the Lord. Paul's example is helpful for us here. In 2 Corinthians 12, Paul talks about the wonderful visions the Lord had granted him, experiences that easily could have led to spiritual arrogance. Paul writes, "So to keep me from becoming proud, I was given a thorn in my flesh, a messenger from Satan to torment me and keep me from becoming proud. Three different times I begged the Lord to take it away. Each time he said, 'My grace is all you need. My power works best in weakness.' So now I am glad to boast about my weaknesses, so that the power of Christ can work through me. That's why I take pleasure in my weaknesses, and in the insults, hardships, persecutions, and troubles that I suffer for Christ. For when I am weak, then I am strong."[3]

To keep him from growing proud, Paul was given a "thorn in the flesh," a factor that brought torment to his life. He asked God three times to remove it. Yet the thorn remained. Paul wasn't delivered from it. His suffering continued. But he wasn't left alone. Instead, he was given grace to endure. His scar became part of his identity, a reminder of his constant need for God's grace. The scar became God's means of perfecting him, of teaching and shaping him through weakness.

Though I hesitate to compare my own experience to the apostle Paul's, I have also experienced the perfecting power of pain. I've seen how God has shaped me through some of my most obvious abnormalities and struggles: the challenge of my multiracial roots, being a minority, witnessing my parents' divorce, my mom's sudden death, failures in the workplace, and broken relationships with my wife, my children, my church, and my friends. These experiences have taught me that God uses all of our story — the pain and struggle — to advance his kingdom.

Another aspect of this maturation is that when we connect with others in community, we discover that it is our particular pain, not our strengths, that enables others to relate to us most intimately. Pain, in this sense, becomes God's gift to us. We all want to make a difference in the world. We all want to connect with others in some way. Pain is the common ground God gives us to meet people, regardless of their cultural background or personal history. People can understand the pain of disappointment, of loss, of failure. Our scars give us the authority through which we can connect to the lives of others. They are the fertile soil where God plants seeds of authenticity, seeds that grow and draw others to the Gardener, the one who can take the dirt and the weeds in our hearts and turn them into a colorful field of blessing.

MARIBEL'S STORY

I recently received an email from a woman named Maribel. It moved me to better understand the beauty that emerges from brokenness. Yet as I read each word, I was also drawn to the rawness of her confession. Maribel is one of my heroes. She is a woman whose dark night has been transformed into the brightness of day. Her life reflects the life of one who has come into the light. If you were to meet her today, you'd be immediately aware of her gentleness. Her experiences of dark betrayal have led to a heightened spiritual sensitivity that inspires those she connects with. She is an ordinary person who lives with a powerful authority because she has embraced her pain and her position as a child of God. God shows through Maribel how he makes all things new. She is one of the purest ones I have ever met. Here is her story:

Pastor Dave,

I've been meaning to write you my story for quite some time now, I just didn't know where to start. First I want to let you know a bit of my background so that you have some idea of how much my life has changed. I was born in Mexico City and was raised in Los Angeles. I am an only child. My mother always said my life was a miracle because the doctors told her she could never conceive a child. When she told them she was pregnant, they thought she was crazy. My father had a previous marriage and could not decide which wife he wanted to keep, so I also have two older stepsisters and a younger stepsister. After I was born, my father left my mother and came to the States. Soon, my mother followed, looking for him, and she left me with my grandmother. My mother and father reunited, but their life was full of abuse and alcohol.

When I was three, they brought me to America with them. As a three-year-old, I began to be emotionally, physically, and sexually abused by my father.

My mother was a great person when she was sober, but she spent most of her life chasing my father into

79

bars, looking for him in the middle of the night. I knew my life was not normal. I had an aunt who tried, over and over again, to take me from my parents. She had six children, and they were like the siblings I never had in my own family. I remember wanting, as a child, to stay with that family. But as I grew older, I ended my relationship with them because they were always pointing out how dysfunctional my parents were, telling me that I would turn out just like them. They were devoted Catholics as well, very strict in their faith, and I rebelled against that.

I started hanging out with several of the most notorious gangsters in the area and started selling drugs in the streets. I began to abuse myself. When I was twelve, cutting myself was a means of comfort; drugs were my escape. I often tried to kill myself. As I grew older, I found a boyfriend who could abuse me, and after he dumped me, I decided that I would start using men. Deep inside, I really hated men . . .

My mother and a friend's father taught me how to prostitute myself. They were my encouragement, and so I eventually started working as a taxi dancer. There I met my first husband, a spoiled, twenty-five-year-old Japanese millionaire. He gave me every material thing I had ever wanted. I had a Porsche, a Mercedes, a house in Corona del Mar overlooking the ocean. I started to love him. But he was clear that he did not want to have children with me, so I had several abortions which sent me into regular cycles of depression. Eventually, he got tired of me and returned to Japan. Again, I tried killing myself and ended up in a recovery home.

When I got out, my life was even darker than my early years. I was hanging out with mafia, and my life was full of drugs and sex. At one point, I wasn't sure if I was gay or if I just hated men. I was in self-destruct mode.

Then, one day at a club in LA, I met a guy named Jason. We were two souls with a lot of sorrow. I could see it written all over him. I fell in love with him, and he cared for me like nobody ever had. He was *honest*. I had never had a guy tell me that he wanted to take me out but he didn't have money! We moved in together, and he let me just be myself, and I loved it. But as the love grew, I got scared because the more I knew him, the more I felt like I did not deserve him. I decided to come clean about my past, and he still wanted to be with me. We planned a wedding, and we got pregnant before the wedding. Our four-month-old daughter was in the wedding! Life was good. I had a second and third child, I started my own business, but inside I was still hearing the enemy telling me to go and kill myself, that I did not deserve happiness. So I would drink to escape confrontations and fears. My marriage grew worse as the years went by. We tried marriage counseling, personal therapists, medications, everything.

At one point, my counselor suggested that I seek a divorce. Instead, I stopped drinking and started helping the homeless and filling my life with work in the hope that it would be the answer I had been looking for. I was as clean as I had ever been, but there was still a great sadness and a heavy burden I carried, almost to the point of suffocation. I thought my only options were divorce or continue pretending I was happy, just to be close to my children. I feared that my husband would take the kids away if I sought divorce because of my rough past. I felt trapped.

One day my friend asked what I wanted to do when my kids were older and had moved out. I thought about it and told her that I'd move to Tibet and find the truth. She laughed and asked me to go to church with her that Sunday. Now, I had gone to churches before and had never really found anything that felt like the truth, so I was very skeptical. But was I ever wrong! That day, you said, "Raise your hand if you want to give your burden to Jesus." You prayed for us and from that day on, my life has been blessed with so many miracles. I found the Truth, and the Truth has set me free! I now feel free to love myself, my husband, my family, and the rest of the world. I am not afraid anymore because Jesus loves me and he is faithful. God has given me a river of living water and my thirst is satisfied in him.

Sola Dei [a prayer ministry] has healed me emotionally and physically. Laundry Love [a community development project to serve the homeless with clean clothes] has taught me about a different kind of love. My children and I have joined BSF [Bible Study Fellowship], and Jason and I recently joined a small group. I am also dedicating more time to helping homeless families and working with several nonprofit organizations.

My life in the last year is nothing like it used to be. I now see the many gifts that God has blessed me with, and I am so excited to share his love with other people. My life was once so dark. Now, it is full of light. It's all from God.

Thank you for being my pastor and for letting God use you in such a beautiful and unique way. God's words from your mouth have saved my life, and those around me say thank you! Tears of gratitude.

Love in Christ,
Maribel

Maribel bravely shared her story at our staff retreat. One of our pastors said the story made her think of Psalm 23. At first, I assumed she was referring to the line about walking through the valley of the shadow of death. But that wasn't what she meant. She quoted the next verse instead: "You honor me by anointing my head with oil. My cup overflows with blessings."[4] I'll never forget her speaking that promise to Maribel. From the seeds of a broken life, God's goodness and mercy now flow. Maribel would be the first to tell you that her life isn't perfect. She manages the tension between her past and her position in Christ every day. But now her past guides her to love the homeless, minister to children, and advocate against human trafficking in Mexico City. Her pain gives her an authority to speak with conviction and power. His strength has become perfected through her weakness. God has used the pain of her past to give us a gift, a person who with gentleness and compassion touches lives in Los Angeles and all over the world.

St. Augustine writes, "In my deepest wound, I see your glory, and it dazzles me."

Our pain becomes the scars for people to see the healing power of our great God. Not only does he heal; he transforms what could have destroyed us.

Our pain becomes our badge of credibility.

Our pain gifts us with authority.

Our pain is our connection to humanity.
Our pain points us toward our destiny.
Ultimately, the last, greatest painful enemy is death itself.
But it has no power over us.
Our pain prepares us for resurrection.
Death is the prelude to new life.

But let me reveal to you a wonderful secret. We will not all die, but we will all be transformed! It will happen in a moment, in the blink of an eye, when the last trumpet is blown. For when the trumpet sounds, those who have died will be raised to live forever. And we who are living will also be transformed. For our dying bodies must be transformed into bodies that will never die; our mortal bodies must be transformed into immortal bodies.

Then, when our dying bodies have been transformed into bodies that will never die, this Scripture will be fulfilled:

"Death is swallowed up in victory.
O death, where is your victory?
O death, where is your sting?"

For sin is the sting that results in death, and the law gives sin its power. But thank God! He gives us victory over sin and death through our Lord Jesus Christ.

So, my dear brothers and sisters, be strong and immovable. Always work enthusiastically for the Lord, for you know that nothing you do for the Lord is ever useless.[5]

God takes what was meant for evil and turns it into good.

5

MYSTERY

the problem with words

The music is meant to be provocative — which doesn't mean it's necessarily obnoxious, but it is (mostly) confrontational, and more than that, it's dense with multiple meanings. Great rap should have all kinds of unresolved layers that you don't necessarily figure out the first time you listen to it. Instead it plants a dissonance in your head. You can enjoy a song that knocks in the club or has witty punch lines the first time you hear it. But great rap retains a mystery. It leaves shit rattling in your head that won't make sense till the fifth or sixth time through. It challenges you.

Which is the other reason hip-hop is controversial: People don't bother trying to get it. The problem isn't the rap or the rapper or the culture. The problem is that so many people don't even know how to listen to the music.

— JAY-Z

IN THIS age of transparency, we expose every gory detail of our lives in public forums, there's a yearning for a pure space, a space to keep certain things unresolved and mysterious. The ancient Celts called this "the thin place," a collision between heaven and earth, where the infinite and the finite, the natural and the supernatural, the tangible and the intangible meet. It's a place of tension, a space where we are free to reclaim a sense of awe—a place of secrets and hidden meanings.

Mystery keeps us engaged, awake and alert, on our toes. It stirs the deep questions of life and invites controversy, yes, but it can also take us to a place of quiet surrender and spiritual inspiration. The thin place, that intangible realm between heaven and earth, is not an easy space to maneuver in, much less to comprehend. We are comfortable with the tangible but are troubled by the unexplained and unknown.

Yet we need mystery just as much as we need the air we breathe.

WHAT DO YOU SAY?

Let's pause a moment to look at a few pictures and jot down a few thoughts.

First, picture yourself standing at the edge of the Grand Canyon.

How would you describe the view?

It's hard to come up with anything that does justice to this wonder of the world.

Now, let's think about love. How do people describe love?

When you are deeply in love with someone, what words do you use to describe how you feel?

Struggling to find the right words?

There are some things words simply cannot fully describe. Saying "I really, really love you" just doesn't do it. Why? Because the awe we experience at the sight of something beautiful and the love we feel in a relationship transcend language. Words fail to convey the depth and breadth of what we experience. In fact, words can cheapen the experience. Sometimes silence is the best response to beauty. Awe leaves us speechless.

Our body language and our actions are often more significant than the words we speak. In school, I studied the art of communication and learned that words make up only ten to twenty percent of our communication. The rest is through our body language, tone, volume, pitch, rate of speaking, perhaps even a vibe we give off. There are experts in the field of communication who are able to determine when a person is lying simply by observing their body language. A friend of mine once demonstrated this ability at a large entertainment company in Hollywood. Those gathered were initially resistant to him and skeptical of his credibility as a consultant. So he spent some time going around the table describing characteristics of every person present. It didn't take long for folks to sit up and listen. His ability to read body language — to decode the unspoken language of those gathered — won him instant credibility as a consultant.

We naturally desire clarity and order. And words can help satisfy that desire. But when we encounter mystery—the more intangible, mystical experiences of life—words seem inadequate. Perhaps you were grieving the loss of a loved one. In moments like that, the worst thing someone can do is fill the quiet with words. Silence is often the most appropriate response. It can be a ministry to others. Our silence provides a sanctuary, creating space to grieve, to reflect, to think, to dream. Silence provides a backdrop, a context for words to be truly heard, and enhances their power when we are ready to listen.

The apostle Paul, who was tutored by the greatest minds of his day and waxed eloquent on Mars Hill when he addressed academics and philosophers, also knew the limitations of words. He wrote to the Corinthian church, reminding them that his message to them came "not with wise and persuasive words, but with a demonstration of the Spirit's power, so that your faith might not rest on human wisdom, but on God's power."[1] Though words are necessary, they are not sufficient. Where the natural and the supernatural meet, something mysterious occurs. God's Spirit moves.

And in partnership with the work of the Holy Spirit, the Bible—God's Word—is uniquely suited to guiding us into truth and wisdom. It is the key to discerning the mysterious ways of God. Every major decision in my life has been informed by meditation on the Scriptures. The Scriptures shed light into the darkness of our lives, providing guidance and direction. "How can a young person stay pure? By obeying your word."[2] The Word of God is clear, and it is the path to a pure life.

Often, institutions and organizations lull us to sleep with excessive dialogue and intellectual eloquence. Even in our interactions with other people, we tend to emphasize what we have to say rather than listening to and responding to the Holy Spirit. Consequently, our prayer times are often hollow and stiff, suffering from the rigor mortis of empty ritual. We entertain one another in the name of spiritual community. We evaluate each other on the basis of words, hypersensitive to the slightest hint of error. In our arguments, words are dissected and heated discussions can be sparked because of a careless word choice. Sadly, we often make snap judgments about a person because they use a certain word, rather than trying to understand what they are communicating. How many lovers have split because they missed what was being communicated, focusing only on what was said, missing the meaning of the heart?

MOM

My mother was killed in a hit-and-run accident. Friends tried to comfort me. They spoke words to address my pain, but they were insufficient. They couldn't address the pain and emptiness I felt. One of the best things my pastor ever did was simply to hold me and sit silently with me, like Job's friends, who sat on the ground with him for seven days, saying nothing to him because they recognized the depth of his suffering. There are times when words are inappropriate.

But it's not just in times of suffering and loss that words are inadequate; they can also fail us when we wish to praise, as we search for a way of comprehending the incomprehensible. The apostle Paul described times in prayer when words were inadequate to express his desire for God: "The Holy Spirit helps us in our weakness. For example, we don't know what God wants us to pray for. But the Holy Spirit prays for us with groanings that cannot be expressed in words."[3] There are times, Paul reminds us, when we lack the words to fully express our needs, and we must rely on the mysterious work of God's Spirit. The apostle Peter describes a similar experience as he considers the joy of knowing Jesus and one day seeing him face to face: "You love him even though you have never seen him. Though you do not see him now, you trust him; and you rejoice with a glorious, inexpressible joy."[4] Our joy in God is inexpressible, Peter tells us, something that cannot be captured by words alone.

Some in the church criticize the gift of speaking in tongues, sometimes referred to as a heavenly language, because it seems unintelligible. Yet those with the gift often share how their unexplainable speaking mysteriously provokes an incomparable level of intimacy with God. Even though they don't understand what they are speaking, many believers report a warming of their hearts by the Spirit of God. Perhaps this is similar to the groanings that Paul speaks of or a way of expressing the inexpressible joy that Peter refers to in his letter. However we interpret these passages, we can be assured that one of the roles of the Spirit is to communicate our inner desires, our deep groanings and longings, to the Father.

As people accustomed to expressing ourselves through words, we may need to counter our dependence on them by embracing a new posture in our approach to God. We may need to retrain ourselves to listen in silence. In our noisy, busy world, we need to carve out space to abide, places for contemplative solitude and quiet meditation. The Bible teaches us to be slow to speak and quick to listen. As we spend time listening, we will discover that there is power in silence, that sitting in quiet wonder and contemplation actually empowers our words with depth and substance. "Silence," as contemplative author Henri Nouwen reminds us, "is the home of the word."

SILENCE AND LISTENING

In his book *The Different Drum*, author Scott Peck discusses four phases of a relationship:

1. The chaotic and antisocial phase
2. The formal and institutional phase
3. The skeptic and individual phase
4. The mystic and communal phase

All relationships move in and out of these four phases. In every relationship, there are seasons of chaos (the chaotic phase), of order (the formal phase), of skepticism (the skeptic phase), and of mystery (the mystic phase). And according to Peck, the mystic phase is the deepest of the phases. This phase is that place of deep communion where two people realize they cannot fully understand everything about each other. Even though they can't make sense of one another, they choose to love. The willingness to accept the unknown, the mystery in the relationship, is a sign of relational maturity.

We attempt to seek understanding in our relationships. In fact, the pursuit of understanding is a driving force in the growth of a relationship. Think of a young man as he pursues his beloved. He is on a quest to understand and to know. Often, in young relationships, the quest for understanding is also a quest to agree — to find commonality and eliminate differences. But there comes a point, after many years, when we realize that it's okay to be different. We may not always agree. It's a tragedy when we can't accept one another because of these differences. True love keeps pursuing understanding, even as it recognizes the beauty of mystery. There is a complex interplay of trust and action, of faith and movement. We continue to seek understanding with others, working toward unity, but we also learn to rest in the simplicity of faith, knowing that there will always be things we do not understand about the other. We learn to trust.

Silence is an expression of trust. The prophet Isaiah writes, "Those who trust in the LORD will find new strength. They will soar high on wings like eagles. They will run and not grow weary. They will walk and not faint."[5] Waiting in stillness and silence demonstrates that we are yielded to God's direction. It is an act of obedience, an opportunity for renewal. The life of a XEALOT is a life of response, following the initiative of God and not our own agendas. But how can we follow if we are preoccupied, distracted by the noise all around us? We learn to watch, wait, and listen.

And as we listen, waiting upon God alone and with others, we find that God speaks to us in a variety of ways. He connects to us through one another, through our families, even through the stranger we meet on the street. He speaks through the uncomfortable moments of our days, as well as through images, dreams, visions, and unlikely circumstances. But most of all, he speaks through his Scriptures. While the written Word of God can seem, at times, incomplete and hard to comprehend, the Bible is clear that it contains everything we need to be made complete.[6] Yet this too is a mystery. Though we meditate upon the Scriptures, and our minds are transformed by the truth, the shaping of our hearts' desires remains a spiritual process, difficult to define. Mysterious. Reading the Scriptures is a dialogue.

The XEALOT life is not always clear and simple. It's a management of tension more than simple solutions. While we embrace the unexplainable, through faith, this does not mean that we acquiesce and do nothing. As James reminds us, faith without works is dead.[7] The thin place is that place in our lives where we connect to the divine, where we step forward to embrace the mystery of faith and live each day in this intersection between heaven and earth. This is the realm where the finite clashes with the infinite, where the limits of our human knowledge meet the necessity for God's supernatural grace.

OVERVALUING CLARITY

I often ask college students, "Where do you see yourself in five years?" Sometimes I get a detailed answer, the five-year plan that includes their career path, a wedding date, and kids' names and genders. Usually, though, their embarrassed reply is the three words that we never want to say: "I don't know."

But when I pose this question, they don't know it's actually a trick question.

"I don't know" is the best possible answer.

One of the lamest things we've done is to convince our young people that they should have their whole lives all figured out. If there's any part of the five-year plan that's not defined, we shame them.

You're not married yet?

You don't have kids yet?

You're changing jobs again?

When are you going to settle down?

To anyone who's in their twenties, let me offer, "Don't worry about it." Think of this decade as the freshman year of your life; it's okay to be undeclared. In fact, it's actually a great place to be. It leaves you open to the possibilities God might have for you.

No matter what age you are, you've got something even better than a five-year plan: open hands. Sit down, open up your hands, and say to God, "Whatever you want me to do, wherever you want me to go, I'm in." When people ask, "Where will you be in five years?" instead of being embarrassed, you can take joy in the fact that it could be anywhere.

> The purpose of a fish trap is to catch fish, and when the fish are caught, the trap is forgotten. The purpose of a rabbit snare is to catch rabbits. When the rabbits are caught, the snare is forgotten. The purpose of words is to convey ideas. When the ideas are grasped, the words are forgotten. Where can I find a man who has forgotten words? He is the one I would like to talk to.
>
> —Chuang Tzu

PART 2

MOVEMENT

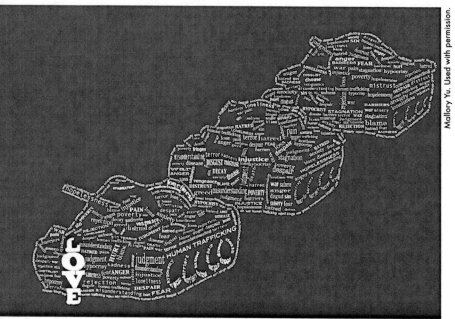

THERE'S an iconic photo from the 1989 Tiananmen Square Massacre in China of a man defiantly standing in the way of a line of tanks.

No one knows who he is, but his stand has inspired millions. Belief catalyzes actions. Those who embrace the XEALOT mind may be sincere in their belief, but until they act, they may be simply dreaming. The way of the XEALOT requires more than a discipline of the mind; a change in our beliefs must lead to movements responding to the Holy Spirit. When a Spirit-filled mind and movement converge, a person becomes a potent force in the hand of God.

As important as beliefs are, our lives are shaped by more than what we believe. Contrarian movements also determine the way we flow in life, the choices we make, the decisions we make on the spur of the moment, beyond the realm of thought. Belief must be wedded to action, mind to movement. This way of life seems like virgin ground. There is One who has walked before us, and he continues to lead the way forward for each generation to respond to his call. He beckons us to follow him on the contrarian path, defying human reason.

The movements of the XEALOT life are not linear or religious. They provoke a flow in our lives, a way of responding that develops as we adhere to the Father's will. More than answers, they are the simplest form of wisdom, insights that hone our navigational skills, making complex decisions seem simple and natural. As we adapt with the Spirit, we learn to rely on the Spirit's power to live out our calling.

When we learn to act on our beliefs, we move beyond the routine and into the abnormal but deeply rich realm of the XEALOT life.

6

OBEDIENCE

the call to die

This is the life I chose, or rather, the life that chose me.
— JAY-Z

When Christ calls a man, he bids him come and die.
— DIETRICH BONHOEFFER

MY FRIEND Dave Brubaker is all passion. We play basketball together. I enjoy our games because he brings it all out on the court. Once, we were playing a two-on-two pickup game, one of those back-and-forth games. Dave did *not* want to lose. Suddenly, the ball was dropped, and it looked like a turnover. But with his usual passion, Dave chased it down, just as an opponent was about to grab it. The only way Dave could guarantee that he would get the ball first was to dive for it. Did I mention that we were playing outside, on an asphalt court? Afterward, Dave's back looked like a pepperoni pizza. As we helped him pick the rocks out of his skin, we laughed at his passion, his willingness to sacrifice his body.

Passion is like a fire inside of you. It's an amazing force in our lives. It can lead to incredible change and motivate people to unparalled feats. But at some point, passion falls short.

We need to be aware of its limitations as well.

When I think of passion, I think of the hare in Aesop's classic tale of the tortoise and the hare. Passion can fill us with a burst of motivation and energy, but it doesn't always enable us to complete the race. In the fable, though the hare takes the early lead, the tortoise crosses the finish line first.

That tortoise is obedience.

Take love, for example. Love is often a pure act of obedience. How many couples decide it's just not worth it during those first few turbulent years of really getting to know each other? How many feel like quitting after the third month of changing diapers every night at 2:00 a.m.?

In trying uninspired moments, passion fails to fuel. Why? And how do we discipline our passion, developing it into the commitment that leads to obedience?

The following are common responses people give for why their passion runs dry.

"I'M JUST NOT FEELING IT ANYMORE"

We make plans, try to choose the career, the relationship, the calling that best fits our gifts, passions, and talents. We examine all the options. Eventually, we choose a particular path.

The problem with this way of thinking is that when we follow God, often our desires are, well, irrelevant. If not irrelevant, it's certainly not the most important factor in determining our purpose. Like a servant or a soldier, sometimes we simply have to accept the assignments we're given.

My friend Dave Brubaker is more than just an insane basketball player. I asked Dave to share this story about a time when he wasn't feeling the passion to work with youth anymore:

> I remember when I first started working at a church, it was a great job, but sometimes it didn't feel very rewarding. Dealing with people can be tiring, and sometimes at the end of the day it's hard to see a return for your labor. I started feeling jealous of people who work in construction. At the end of the day, they have something tangible that they can point to and say, "I did that."
>
> Ironically, I am probably the least handy person in the world. I can't even put up a shelf without having it end up crooked. Yet I still had this fantasy in my mind: "If I could do anything, I would work in construction."
>
> One day, I came home to my apartment complex and saw some guys doing a renovation on one of the buildings. As I got out of my car, one of the workers walked by. I couldn't resist making a comment.
>
> "Man, you've got the best job in the world."
>
> He stopped, then asked me, "What do you do?"
>
> "Oh, I work at the church down the street."
>
> He seemed a little puzzled and challenged me. "You do an important job like that, and you're jealous of my work?"
>
> I felt kind of sheepish. I had just been making polite conversation, and suddenly he was calling me out. Then the conversation took a crazy turn. He said, "When you get home, get your Bible and look up 2 Timothy 2:4, see what it says."
>
> The construction worker giving the pastor a verse to look up? But after I got home and read it, I was stunned. No joke, I think the guy may have actually been an angel sent

to teach me a lesson. Here's what the verse said: "No one serving as a soldier gets involved in civilian affairs; he wants to please his commanding officer."

Whether he was an angel or just the most theologically profound man ever to pick up a hammer, the lesson was clear. God didn't want to hear me talk about construction anymore. I was a soldier and I had an assignment, and even if there were other things I wanted to do, my real job was to please my commanding officer. Whether I was "feeling it" or not.

Our sense of passion can be misleading. Far more important is our willingness to serve, our openness to God's direction, and our submission to his leading.

"I HAVE NOTHING TO OFFER"

This excuse is the tag team of "I'm just not feeling it." Tag team member 1 typically hits you when your circumstances no longer inspire you. The powerful emotion or the initial excitement has been replaced by tolerance and the ordinary routine.

Tag team member 2 hits you when the well within runs dry.

Any great endeavor worth pursuing will stir up these questions about your abilities or lack thereof.

At some point in life, we all reach this stage. You set out to do something great, believing that you have ideas to contribute, work to do, insights to uncover that no one has ever heard before. Just a bit of wisdom, some creativity, and a fresh idea will soon put you at the front of the pack.

Then, you experience a setback. People aren't excited about your ideas. You disappoint that person whose opinion means the world to you. Or you start working alongside someone who is ten times better than you are. Afterward, all you can do is sit. You feel dead inside. Passionless. Defeated.

It's a nauseating feeling. But in moments like these we become open to God and his Word in a unique way. During a personal crisis, God led me to Psalm 51, which was written by King David after perhaps the biggest failure of his life. David wrote this to God:

> You do not desire a sacrifice, or I would offer one.
> You do not want a burnt offering.
> The sacrifice you desire is a broken spirit.
> You will not reject a broken and repentant heart,
> O God.[1]

There are two ways we can say "I have nothing to offer." One is the cry of frustration, as we look to ourselves in bitterness and despair. The other is the cry of a broken heart, looking for restoration, calling out to God in weakness. Though I felt passionless in the moment when I finally came to God, I felt like he was saying, "Dave, I've been waiting a long time for you to get here." I sensed that day that God was not interested in reigniting red-hot passion in me, a passion that is here today and gone tomorrow. He was interested in breaking my heart, preparing me to obey.

THE ROAD JESUS TRAVELED

John 12:27–28 gives us a window into the way Jesus processed his emotions, the troubling thoughts that threatened to overwhelm him as he looked to the cross, the pain and suffering that awaited him: "Now my soul is deeply troubled. Should I pray, 'Father, save me from this hour'? But this is the very reason I came! Father, bring glory to your name."

Here we see Jesus in anguish. He gives us an opportunity to listen in on his thoughts. Like most of us, he knows the normal desire to be delivered from a difficult situation. We too wrestle with God's calling on our lives. We are tempted to pray that God would artfully place us in a space that's easier, a situation that we can feel passionate about. We want to do something that we feel really matters.

But Jesus rejects that option. He doesn't pray for the Father to save him from the journey to the cross. Why? Because Jesus knows that even if it is difficult, even if it leads to pain and suffering, this is the assignment he was born to complete. The passion of Jesus *is* his suffering. His example proves that godly passion is born not of our desires but in the difficult path of obedience, where our lives bring glory to God.

DAD

Recently, my dad passed away. As you might imagine, we had a volatile relationship after he left our family. Much of this was my own fault. But over the years, my heart toward my father changed. At first, I began reconnecting with him simply as an act of defiance. There was no passion, no desire to know him or understand him. But as I moved toward him in obedience to God, I began to see my dad in new ways, through a new set of eyes. I began to see him as Gary, not just my dad but a man like me, broken and human. Slowly I began to see my own sin and hypocrisy. I saw how easy it was for me to throw stones and ignore my failures in the relationship. I saw, in a fresh way, God's grace in my life.

Though I am rebellious, he still pursues me.
He still loves me.

MORE THAN A FEELING

Rodney Stark, a church historian, wondered why Christianity grew with such speed during its early years. And as he studied, he uncovered an interesting truth: when pandemics occurred, people fled the disease-filled city, leaving behind the suffering and dying. But the Christians stayed behind, caring for the victims, putting their own health at risk. These were clearly acts of love. They were not decisions to make their own lives happier or more convenient. They were not decisions driven by temporary feelings or concerns. They were rooted in God-inspired compassion.

True love is a radical act of sacrifice, trusting God to catalyze and sustain change. Following Jesus involves our passion, but it is more than transient feelings. It's about trusting the Father enough that we follow his calling and walk in obedience to him even when we don't fully understand his ways.

Sacrificial obedience defines the XEALOT life. It's a contrarian path. Jesus taught and modeled this way of life for us. Consider how he taught us to act. Remember, this is not just something we believe but is the way we live. Jesus defines a new movement, something he not only believed but also lived out through suffering and death on a cross. He taught us:

"Love your enemies."[2]
"Bless those who persecute you. Don't curse them; pray that
God will bless them."[3]
"Love your neighbor as yourself."[4]
"Take up your cross, and follow me."[5]

"You are no longer part of the world."[6]
"Forgive others, and you will be forgiven."[7]

Following Jesus is about more than good feelings, a prosperous life, and calling him your good buddy. It's about obedience to these imperatives. Yes, joy is a part of the journey, but like any relationship, there will be highs and lows, moments of frustration and disappointment. Still, in the end, following Jesus is less a matter of knowing our passion, our inner desire, that thing that makes us feel fulfilled and happy. It's actually the opposite of the self-directed life. It's learning to die, each day, in obedience to God's will and his purpose for our lives.

> He humbled himself in obedience to God
> and died a criminal's death on a cross.
> — PHILIPPIANS 2:8

7

NATURALLY
SUPERNATURAL

unleashing beauty

I will pour out my Spirit upon all people. Your sons and daughters will prophesy. Your old men will dream dreams, and your young men will see visions. In those days I will pour out my Spirit even on servants — men and women alike.

—JOEL 2:28–29

SUPERMAN.

Batman.

Power Rangers.

X-Men.

Judging by the popularity of our favorite superheroes, it's not a stretch to say that something in us connects with these fictitious beings with exceptional powers. We are fascinated by what is beyond us, by the notion of a supernatural life, a life beyond the ordinary. And our desire for this transcendent life goes beyond a fascination with comic books. It's a deeply rooted longing for another world.

The writer of Ecclesiastes pens, "He has planted eternity in the human heart."[1] Eternity, as the book of Ecclesiastes goes on to say, is a natural yearning to experience the supernatural, a desire for the transcendent and the divine. Unfortunately, we all too readily fill this vacuum in our hearts with superficial substitutes. Things that don't matter—in light of eternity—easily become priorities that temporarily satisfy our craving for something bigger than us, the life that eludes us.

We eventually settle for normality: the regular path of satisfying our longing for transcendence. We try to get away on weekends. We long to escape the humdrum reality of our routines. Or we satisfy our longing through entertainment. Fiction books are more popular than ever, soap operas inspire us, comic books fill our imagination, and gaming gives us the temporary thrill of risk. This is our outlet for excitement, for adventure. It's fueled by a God-given thirst for something more, a heavenly high that is intrinsic to each one of us.

We also know that these attempts are not real. They don't last. We hunger for food, yet we settle for cotton candy. We reach for the quick fix, but we discover that it has a nasty aftertaste. It rots our dreams and fails to satisfy, leaving us wanting more.

TOUCHING HEAVEN

What if we, like the people in the Bible, personally experienced God through dreams, visions, miracles, and supernatural circumstances? Probably few of us have heard God speaking audibly. While some may have had a vision or experienced a miracle, it doesn't happen every day. Instead, God chooses to communicate in gentle, unassuming ways. He speaks in a way that is difficult to perceive but still can be felt and discerned.

I believe it's possible for each of us—not just spiritual leaders—to experience the furious love of God through the Holy Spirit. God desires to reveal himself to us through the supernatural and the miraculous, in ways that are unimaginable. When my wife and I are asked how people can pray for us, we ask them to pray that our children experience God. God may do great things in our lives, but we don't want our children simply to see what God does in *our* lives. We want them to experience his miracles for themselves. We want them to richly encounter God.

We know that God is moving, doing his work in amazing ways. We hear stories from the East or from the Global South, stories of God's spiritual fire burning, stories of miracles and supernatural healings. If you've spent any time traveling or speaking with Christians in other countries, you've likely heard about the ways God is moving on those continents. The miraculous is the norm in many places.

I can vouch for this. I've seen it. It's true. And it's beautiful. But what about the West? Why don't we see these moves of God? I believe a new day is rising, a day when we'll experience firsthand the supernatural work of God. Already, we are seeing unprecedented moves of God in many major cities in North America: Los Angeles, Santa Ana, New York, Chicago, Portland, Seattle, Vancouver, Toronto, Dallas, and Miami. We're also hearing reports of God's moving in the Nazareths of the West, those little-known, quiet places, the smaller cities, the suburbs, and the rural communities.

As we look back at the spiritual movements of the past, we gain perspective on the present. Many of the most significant spiritual awakenings began in lesser-known places. Places like Azusa, California, where the Pentecostal movement began at the start of the twentieth century. The rise of camp meetings in small towns along the east coast of the United States. Or the spiritual influence of the International House of Prayer in Kansas City. The Vineyard movement, pioneered by John Wimber in the late 1970s, began in Anaheim, California. None of these places were considered centers of global influence at the time. If you are from a small, unrecognized place, don't worry. Just like Jesus and his band of XEALOTS, God is raising up followers in unknown places all over the world.

What about your own life? Have you considered the truth that God desires to give *you* the supernatural gifts of the Spirit? These are Spirit-empowered gifts that can equip you to do things outside of what may be considered normal.

What if we could leave behind the fantasy and taste the reality of the supernatural?

I believe we can.

GETTING UNFROZEN AT THE FROZEN YOGURT PLACE

I was at a frozen yogurt hot spot, and a strange thing happened. As I was picking up my yogurt from the counter, a young friend of mine suddenly felt moved to pray for me. We walked outside onto the busy sidewalk and he turned to face me, putting his hands on my shoulders. Right there, in the midst of the crowd, he started praying, loudly and emotionally, oblivious to the people walking by or those who had stopped to stare at us. I'll be honest, I was embarrassed. I realized that I was more concerned about what people thought about me than about experiencing the power of the Holy Spirit. One of the biggest challenges we face when using the gifts that God gives us is overcoming our fear of what others think. By definition, the gifts are extraordinary and gracious. They are supernatural. At times, they seem very strange. The gifts invite us to appear childish—even foolish—to experience the wonderful work of the Holy Spirit. Paul, in prison, pens to his spiritual son, Timothy, "For God has not given us a spirit of fear and timidity, but of power, love, and self-discipline."[2] This fear-rejecting power is found in the person of the Holy Spirit. Perfect love will cast out any fear.

In Acts 2 and Ephesians 5:18, we find references to the power of the Holy Spirit. Acts 2 describes when people first experienced this power, and it tells us that those who were watching thought that the believers were loaded on alcohol. Again, in Ephesians 5:18, Paul makes a similar comparison between a life full of the Spirit and a person filled with spirits of a different kind. He writes, "Don't be drunk with wine, because that will ruin your life. Instead, be filled with the Holy Spirit." In other words, there is something about being filled with the Holy Spirit that is comparable to being drunk! Some of the very same things that people look for from a can of beer are actually sustainable characteristics of a life filled with the Spirit. The apostle Paul tells us that alcohol is a physical imitation of a spiritual reality that God gives us in the Holy Spirit. Being filled with the Spirit can lead to a loss of our inhibitions, a sense of freedom to be ourselves, the confidence to pray loudly when we're standing in front of a yogurt shop. Alcohol is the cheap substitute. It may momentarily quench our thirst and may make us feel good but leaves us dehydrated and hung over. But drinking deeply of the Spirit doesn't dehydrate us. The Spirit is a source of living water, a fountain of life that God can use to quench the thirst of others.[3]

BANGKOK DREAMS

Like *Los Angeles*, the word *Bangkok* means "city of angels." Every year, the prime minister of Thailand prays for the spirits to visit Thailand. Having lived in Bangkok (and LA) with my family, I've seen firsthand that spirits really do come when invited! As an international destination and the gateway to Asia, Bangkok is home to intense spiritual activity.

Several months prior to moving to Bangkok, I experienced some vivid, powerful dreams while sleeping. Often, I felt like I was choking and about to die. I would wake up with a sense that if I had waited a moment longer, I would have been gone. It felt as if someone was suffocating me in my bed. Even after we arrived in Bangkok and throughout our stay, I had several more experiences like this, as did other members of our team. As we talked and prayed, we felt certain that this was the work of evil

spirits, a phenomenon that is not all that strange in Southeast Asia. After I returned home, the experiences gradually stopped, and since then I have often wondered why. Why is it that we rarely see such obvious spiritual activity in the West?

Often, I wonder if Satan's strategy is different for us here in the West. Why create fear and spiritual bondage through displays of spiritual power when he can just as easily — if not more effectively — keep us bound through addictions to amusements, greed, intellectualism, and reliance on our own creativity, all things that can easily replace a reliance on the power of the Holy Spirit?

During our time in Bangkok, even as we encountered spiritual beings, we sensed the Holy Spirit moving, demonstrating his love and graceful force in response to our prayers for help. We witnessed miraculous healings and felt God's comforting, guiding presence in our lives. Despite the attacks at night, I longed for more of God. God used this time in Southeast Asia to deconstruct many of my preconceived notions of the Holy Spirit, showing me his practical care in the midst of spiritual attacks. This was a power I wasn't used to leaning into.

AN ABNORMAL SUNDAY MORNING

I recall another time when one of my friends, a twentysomething young man named Jaeson, received a divine impression for me and for our church. He believed that God was telling him that many people would be healed at our church. People would come for healing from all around the world. I believe Jaeson has a fresh and beautiful connection with God, and he communicates with an endearing rawness, so I asked him to speak at our church. Before the service, Jaeson told me that he had a dream and believed that many people would come forward that day to receive healing. He also saw a vision of people surrounding the platform, committing their lives to God. He had envisioned a wind as well, gently blowing them forward to commit themselves to God.

After Jaeson finished speaking that morning, he looked at me and told me that he felt a severe pain in his arm. He came to me holding his hurting arm, slightly hunched over, and said, "Man, this hurts." He had no idea why he was feeling pain or where it had come from. He was about to ask me up to take over, to give an invitation for people to come forward for prayer and to receive Christ, when he felt a strong sense that someone else in the room needed healing for one of their arms. He felt certain that God had given him this pain so that others would be encouraged to step forward and receive healing that day. So he asked, right then, if anyone had a problem with pain in their arm.

A young man who had recently started attending our church raised his hand. Jaeson stepped down and approached him, and then prayed a simple prayer: "God, heal his arm." And God healed him, right there.

All of this was happening right before my eyes. Everyone was watching what was happening. Jaeson asked, "Would anyone else like prayer?" The aisles filled with people. Jaeson then received an insight that someone had almost died the night before, adding that God had spared his life to give him the opportunity to follow him again. Now it just so happened that this individual was one of my closest friends. He too stepped forward during the invitation and shared that he had been driving down the freeway and had almost missed his off-ramp. Without thinking, he had swerved his car over and failed to see that there was a curb blocking his way. The car struck the curb at high speed, blowing out two tires. The vehicle came to a screeching halt. He shared that he knew at that moment that God had spared his life. After Jaeson called him up for prayer, my friend told me, "Dave, that was me who got in the accident last night. I easily could have died. My car should have flipped multiple times. And man, when Jaeson spoke about someone dying, I felt this wind blowing me forward. I looked up and around me and there were no air conditioning vents, but I still felt a wind. It was blowing me forward."

I'm convinced that God's Spirit is alive and moving in our midst. He wants to give us more than a taste of eternity; he wants to lavish his love on us.

Supernatural.

That Sunday-morning experience forever changed my life, as well as the life of our church. We now believe in and welcome the mysterious work of the Holy Spirit to move among us. I'll be honest, I'm still scratching the surface, learning new things about the movement of God's Spirit each day. But I do know this: when I worship today, I worship not only the Father and the Son but also God the Holy Spirit, who wants to inspire our churches and quench our thirst with something better than wine.

Experiences like the ones I've shared have altered my prayer life as well. No longer do I pray in a monologue, simply asking God for things I need and want. Prayer is dynamic, a dialogue in which we anticipate meeting with God. Prayer is a time when God engages us, revealing things to us and healing us. Time with him transforms our hearts and minds to become one with his.

As Christians, we can easily get caught up in the path of normality. We follow the safe path of the Christian life, talking about the Holy Spirit and doing things to keep busy. Yet do we live in his power? Matthew, one of Jesus' first disciples, reminds us of Christ's words: "The gateway to life is very narrow and the road is difficult, and only a few ever find it."[4] It's easy to miss the narrow path of obedience when our lives are filled with dazzling distractions, many of them now a part of the "normal" Christian life.

My friend Francis once shared a message about our need to embrace a radical understanding of our calling to follow God, to avoid the path of normality. "There is no middle road," said Francis. He compared our response to God to his daughter's hypothetical response to his request that she clean her room. What if his daughter were to come back to him, several hours later, to let him know that even though she hadn't cleaned the room, she had memorized everything he had said to her. That's not obedience, is it? It's disobedience, and yet it illustrates the way we often respond to God's will in our lives. What if, after several more hours, his daughter were to come back again and tell him that though she *still* had not cleaned the room, she had done some further study on what he had said and knew what it really means in the Greek. Yes, there is plenty of activity and even some study happening, but the room stays the same — untouched. In a similar way, Francis suggested, many of us are numbed by the anesthetic of busyness while really doing nothing to follow Jesus.

The apostle Paul once warned Timothy to keep an eye out for people like this. He wrote, "They will act religious, but they will reject the power that could make them godly."[5] I like the way some other translations say it as well: "having a form of godliness but denying its power" (NIV). An essential part of living God's calling is leaning into the Holy Spirit, not relying on human strength. We must learn to be led, rather than leading ourselves.

PRAYER PARTIES

Prayer and *party* are two words that don't seem congruent, right? But that's what my friend Bill did when he dubbed our prayer gatherings "prayer parties," and the name has stuck to this day. We began meeting in homes and hotel rooms for extended periods of time to pray. After one of these times (about seven hours that felt like just a few minutes), Bill exclaimed to all of us there, "This is a prayer *party!*" I now try to regularly join some of these spontaneous prayer parties, times when we simply pray for people, for God to fill us and speak to us. We gather in a room, invite the Holy Spirit to engage us. We ask that he'll reveal to us images, insights, words, and Scripture we need to digest. I've seen businesspeople, housewives, creative artists, and students joining together, hungry for prayer. One can see the warmth of love radiating from everyone after the prayer gathering is over, a sign that many have been inebriated with the Holy Spirit.

Why do I share this? My hope is that you will be inspired to throw spontaneous prayer parties. You don't need to plan them. You will need to pay attention to the leading of the Holy Spirit. Look for situations in which he might be leading you to pray for people—when you're at a party, at a lunch appointment, at a dinner gathering, even at a concert. When you sense that God might be prompting you, simply ask the person if they'd like prayer. If they agree, gently lay hands on them, with their permission. Be open to the possibility that the Holy Spirit will reveal things to you about those who are present. Sometimes you may feel like sharing something, while at other times, you can just start praying for them without preaching at them or prophesying. Your prayer doesn't have to be very long; just ask God to heal, reveal, affirm, lead, and speak. Remember that the purpose of praying for others is to encourage them and to build them up. While many of your prayers might be fairly simple, you should expect to experience some crazy images or thoughts as well. Remember that everything is open to the scrutiny of the Scriptures and the affirmation of those around you. I suggest that when you sense that a word or image might be from God, you avoid saying, "God said this." Instead, be cautious and humbly say, "I *believe* that God *may* be saying this."

Joel states, quite plainly, that there will come a season of an outpouring of the Holy Spirit, a time when dreams and visions will be unleashed among God's people. "I will pour out my Spirit upon all people. Your sons and daughters will prophesy. Your old men will dream dreams, and your young men will see visions. In those days I will pour out my Spirit even on servants—men and women alike."[6] I believe that season began with the giving of the Holy Spirit at Pentecost and is still happening today. The time is now. The move of God could be loud, but it often reflects his character of gentleness and joy.

THE "SPILLING" OF THE SPIRIT

How can we experience what Joel prophesied in our lives and in our churches today? Here are four suggestions:

1. *Jump.* This is such a simple first step, but it's essential. I often hear people, including church leaders, telling others that they need to pray harder and longer, multiple hours per day. But how long we pray isn't always the real problem. If we really believe in the power of the Holy Spirit, it changes everything. No one will have to tell you that you need to pray or how long you should pray. If we really believe that the Holy Spirit is who the Bible says he is, nothing is more exciting than praying. Prayer

becomes less of a work to beg God to do something and more of an ongoing conversation.

2. *Ask the Holy Spirit to take over your life completely.* There are no formulas for experiencing God's work in your life. Start by asking in the name of Jesus to experience the Spirit. And be ready to receive the gifts God has for you, whenever and however he chooses to give them.

3. *Passionately pursue the Holy Spirit.* Don't just ask once. Keep at it. Plan to spend time regularly with God. You will soon begin discerning the Holy Spirit's voice in your life. As you follow him and obey what the Spirit says to you through the Word of God, you will gain authority and power by the Spirit. Ask him to give you his eyes, his dreams, and his vision for your life, for others, and for the world.

4. *Fasting.* To experience intimacy with the Spirit, we must seek times of silence and solitude. It's a space that we're not used to. This seeking can involve the practice of fasting or "lent." You might find it helpful to abandon various forms of media for a time. A media fast is a special type of fast, unique to our age and culture, that can help us to hear again, freed from the distracting noise all around us. My daughter and her friend actually did a mirror and makeup fast!

Finally, spend some time reflecting on the beautiful chaos of the unleashing of God's Spirit on the day of Pentecost:

On the day of Pentecost all the believers were meeting together in one place. Suddenly, there was a sound from heaven like the roaring of a mighty windstorm, and it filled the house where they were sitting. Then, what looked like flames or tongues of fire appeared and settled on each of them. And everyone present was filled with the Holy Spirit and began speaking in other languages, as the Holy Spirit gave them this ability.

At that time there were devout Jews from every nation living in Jerusalem. When they heard the loud noise, everyone came running, and they were *bewildered* to hear their own languages being spoken by the believers.

They were completely *amazed*. "How can this be?" they exclaimed....

They stood there *amazed* and *perplexed*. "What can this mean?" they asked each other.

But others in the crowd ridiculed them, saying, "They're just *drunk*, that's all!"[7]

Bewildered.

Amazed.

Perplexed.

Drunk.

We don't always understand when God's Spirit moves. But the Bible tells us that God is not the author of confusion,[8] that our meetings need to be done decently and in order.[9] God wisely plans what he does and is not random, even though he might seem that way. What may look perplexing to us might have been meticulously orchestrated by God.

Let me invite you to stop reading and to pray — right now — that God will speak to you and reveal himself to you in a supernatural way. Pray that God will speak through his Word, through his people, through your circumstances, even through dreams and visions! And be prepared. What can seem bewildering at first just might be a revelation from God.

8

BECOMING A FATHER

He ran to his son, embraced him, and kissed him.

— LUKE 15:20

I DON'T know if you were all that interested in your high school yearbook, but I can't forget the anticipation I had the day mine was released. As soon as it was in my possession, I raced through the pages. Why? I wasn't looking for my favorite teacher or that snapshot of the principal on the first page. I wasn't even interested in what my friends looked like.

No. I was looking for myself, Numero Uno, the Big Kahuna, me!

In fact, immediately after finding my class picture, I flipped to the index of names to find all of the places in the book where my mug could be found — the sports teams and extracurricular activities I had been involved in. I scrutinized every photograph of me.

I don't think I was all that unique in wanting to see myself *first.*

We all see the world this way. We put ourselves first. We see ourselves at the center of most things.

The default worldview we are all born with places "me" at the center. We all know it's true. Our relationships reveal this over time. We think of ourselves first. We focus on meeting our needs before those of others. But there is something wrong with this way of living, especially as we experience the love of Christ.

Jesus once told a story about a family: a father who had two sons. And in this story, we learn something about ourselves, about God, and about the kind of people God wants us to become. We learn what it means to be a son and what it means to become like the father—to transition from the mindset of a selfish son to a generous father.

> A man had two sons. The younger son told his father, "I want my share of your estate now before you die." So his father agreed to divide his wealth between his sons.
>
> A few days later this younger son packed all his belongings and moved to a distant land, and there he wasted all his money in wild living. About the time his money ran out, a great famine swept over the land, and he began to starve. He persuaded a local farmer to hire him, and the man sent him into his fields to feed the pigs. The young man became so hungry that even the pods he was feeding the pigs looked good to him. But no one gave him anything.
>
> When he finally came to his senses, he said to himself, "At home even the hired servants have food enough to spare, and here I am dying of hunger! I will go home to my father and say, 'Father, I have sinned against both heaven and you, and I am no longer worthy of being called your son. Please take me on as a hired servant.'"

So he returned home to his father. And while he was still a long way off, his father saw him coming. Filled with love and compassion, he ran to his son, embraced him, and kissed him. His son said to him, "Father, I have sinned against both heaven and you, and I am no longer worthy of being called your son."

But his father said to the servants, "Quick! Bring the finest robe in the house and put it on him. Get a ring for his finger and sandals for his feet. And kill the calf we have been fattening. We must celebrate with a feast, for this son of mine was dead and has now returned to life. He was lost, but now he is found." So the party began.

Meanwhile, the older son was in the fields working. When he returned home, he heard music and dancing in the house, and he asked one of the servants what was going on. "Your brother is back," he was told, "and your father has killed the fattened calf. We are celebrating because of his safe return."

The older brother was angry and wouldn't go in. His father came out and begged him, but he replied, "All these years I've slaved for you and never once refused to do a single thing you told me to. And in all that time you never gave me even one young goat for a feast with my friends. Yet when this son of yours comes back after squandering your money on prostitutes, you celebrate by killing the fattened calf!"

His father said to him, "Look, dear son, you have always stayed by me, and everything I have is yours. We had to celebrate this happy day. For your brother was dead and has come back to life! He was lost, but now he is found!"[1]

In most English Bibles, this story is titled the parable of the "Prodigal Son" or the "Lost Son." But it's really a story about a father with two sons. The younger son asks for his share of the estate, prior to the death of his father. The father graciously agrees to divide his belongings, giving a share to the younger son, who leaves home for a distant land. There the son squanders his wealth. He hits rock bottom. He takes a job feeding pigs but isn't able to earn enough to feed himself. Eventually, he decides to return home. Upon his return, the father responds to him with gracious love and acceptance, forgiving him and restoring him to his place in the family.

The older brother, however, is angry at the father's response, bitter at the perceived injustice of it all. So when the father learns of this, he meets with his older son. He responds with loving correction, revealing a heart of merciful compassion and generosity for both sons.

So who is the central figure in this story? Is it the younger son? The older brother? No, this isn't a story about a wayward son or a frustrated older brother. It's a story about an unusually generous and wise father. It should be titled "The Beautiful Father."

THE BEAUTIFUL FATHER

Leighton Ford, a brother-in-law of Billy Graham and a respected Christian leader, was a rising star among Christian leaders. He was regularly invited to speak to thousands of people at events all around the world. But when his son, Sandy, died, Dr. Ford surprised everyone by shifting the focus of his work. He stepped away from the crowds, from the limelight and his work with big-name organizations. And out of his pain, God guided him to begin a leadership-development initiative, working with small groups of young leaders. Somehow, I was chosen to be among his first group, the guinea pigs of this new program. We were really nothing but a band of misfits. In many ways, this opportunity was an answer to my prayers. I had been asking God for a group of godly sages to speak into my life.

During our first gathering, Leighton challenged us to spend some time each day meditating on a painting by Rembrandt titled *The Return of the Prodigal Son*. You can find this famous painting hanging in the Hermitage in St. Petersburg, Russia. I have a print of it in my office. It wonderfully captures the moment in Jesus' parable when the son meets the father and falls at his feet, crying out for mercy.

We spent a week looking at the painting during our morning reflection time, absorbing the multiple hues, the lines, and the nuances of the work. Then, after we had meditated on the

Rembrandt, *The Return of the Prodigal Son*

painting, Dr. Ford would look at each of us with his penetrating eyes and peer into our souls.

"Gaze at this painting. What do you see?" he would ask.

The painting depicts several men. Three of them are given prominence by the lighting and the contrast of the painting. In the foreground, we see the father and the prodigal son himself, kneeling before the father. We see the older brother standing off to the side, unhappy with his father's extension of grace.

"When you look at this picture," Leighton asked us, "who do you most identify with? Who are you in this picture?"

Most of us relate to the prodigal son. We envision ourselves in his place, being embraced by the loving arms of the father. Remember that the real story is not the pride of the prodigal. The focus of the story is the radical generosity of the father. He's the highlight. He represents the heart of God. He is the one we need to learn to identify with as we mature in God's grace. When you look at the painting, you see that Rembrandt understood this. He got it right.

The light in the painting is arranged so that the greatest amount falls on the father, almost radiating from him. The father recognizes his wandering son, even from a distance. Both the parable and the painting highlight a unique attribute of the father. Instead of responding from a desire for retribution, the father chooses to bless his son. Even before the son asks for forgiveness, the father has already forgiven him.

Though we naturally relate to the son in this story, perhaps the real point is that we must become like the father. Jesus uses this story to expose our hearts, to show us how God responds to people and to invite us to respond similarly with generous love. Each of us who follow Jesus must make a shift in our identity from the heart of the son to the heart of the father, from being a person who seeks their own good to a person who freely gives to others, a person of blessing.

Perhaps this is the greatest movement of life. The movement from receiving to blessing, from son to father.

SEEING AND BLESSING

One Sunday, as I scanned the people gathered that morning for worship, I was struck by how easy it is to walk into our church and not be noticed. I wondered how many of the people I saw were longing for some type of human touch. I thought about how hard it is to really connect. We each long for others to see our souls, our true selves, and respond with love and acceptance. Do husbands really see their wives? Do children really know their dads?

I travel to New York City about once a month. I see the same thing as I watch people walking by on the street. In Manhattan, I see people who are talking on their phones or texting others. Each is blind to the people right in front of them. Do we really see each other? Do we take time to notice the people we spend time with? When was the last time you felt like someone really understood you? When did someone look into your soul?

When I look at my kids, I stare at them in amazement. They're beautiful. But often, they don't see the same things I see.

I remember when I gave several speeches back in my high school days. My mom usually just sat stoically in the audience. In most Asian cultures, parents avoid complimenting their children or giving them too much attention if they are being honored. But this one time, I remember noticing her eyes change as I walked to the front. I saw her eyes following me. Her eyes brightened, she sat up straight, and the tears began to flow.

She didn't have to say a word. I knew she was proud of me. As I was delivering my speech, I sensed her favor and love.

Few things are more satisfying than sensing that you are favored, that you are loved and known by someone. Someone sees your soul and they delight in you. They believe in you, believe that what you do will change lives. And that's what empowers those who know Jesus. We are seen by God for who we really are. In Jesus we are deeply known and loved, welcomed by the Father, and adopted into his family. When God sees us, he knows us, and his way of relating to us changes us. It sparks a new rhythm in our lives, a transition that shifts our hearts from the heart of a selfish son to the heart of a generous father. We come as needy children. Our hearts are filled and transformed. We mature and grow as our love for others expands.

Our world today desperately needs fathers. The current generation of youth is largely fatherless. They are crying out to anyone who will listen, "Do you see me? Do I matter to you?" They have never had anyone affirm them. They have never had a father call out their gifts and recognize their special destiny. As followers of Jesus, we are uniquely able to give them the blessing of the Father. But it all begins by learning to see people, really see them as God does, as beautiful, recognizing who God has destined them to be.

Imagine for a moment that God is dreaming about you. He laughs with you. His eyes are filled with joy as he watches you during your daily routine. His heart is filled with a mixture of thrill, joy, and pride, just like a father and a mother who watch their children take their first steps. He is proud when you belt out that solo, show kindness to a stranger, or seek to desperately know him. Our Father delights in us. The psalmist tells us that God's thoughts are vast, outnumbering the grains of sand,[2] and that he perceives our thoughts and knows our words, even before we speak: "O Lord, you have examined my heart and know everything about me."[3] When God sees us, he knows us in a way that doesn't lead to fear of being rejected or punished. He sees us and knows us, yet in that knowing, we sense that we are covered by his love and acceptance.

THE KISS OF GOD

We first learn to share the blessing of the father as we see people through eyes filled with generous love. Growing as a father who blesses others involves a "kiss." The Gospels tell us that Jesus received a kiss from one of his disciples on the night he was betrayed, the kiss of Judas, a kiss of betrayal and duplicity. But the "kiss" of God is altogether different. It's an overflow of his generous love. It is unlike the selfish kisses we receive from others, kisses that have hidden agendas and seek to manipulate. No, the kiss of God is filled with great affection and intimacy, stirring us to even greater love. The kiss of God never stops.

In the story of the beautiful father and his wayward son in Luke 15, we see an Eastern father rising above cultural norms to share his love with his son. Some consider this one of the most intimate texts in the Bible, when understood in the cultural context of Jesus' day. The younger son arrogantly asks his father for his share of the inheritance. When does a son normally receive his inheritance? When the father dies. This brash son is saying to his father, "I wish you were dead. Just give me what I deserve." This is an insult to the father, a terrible dishonor. As knowledge of the son's offense likely spread around the neighborhood, the son would have found himself despised and unwelcome.

Yet upon the son's return, when the father first sees him on the horizon, what does the father do? "He ran to his son, embraced him, and kissed him."[4] The father runs. This is a furious love that doesn't wait for us to come home. It's a love that comes to us, flouting societal norms. Respected authority figures typically did not run in that culture. The father runs to his son, disgracing himself in front of the neighbors. He doesn't give him a tentative shake of the hand or a peck on the cheek. The father unashamedly, in a full chest-to-chest embrace, engulfs his son. He gives his son a big wet one! And not just one. The "kiss" of the father is in the iterative tense in the original Greek, meaning that this is something he does repeatedly, kissing him over and over again. He can't stop kissing his son.

What is the "kiss" of the father? As understood in relation to our Father God, the "kisses" are those supernatural touches we receive from God, those regular reminders of his forgiveness, tenderness, and faithfulness. They are the signs we see in our lives that remind us of his radical generosity, his hope for our lives, his love for us, and his unspeakable joy in saving and welcoming us.

There are clues in the story that the wayward son was nervous about coming home. He knew he had failed, that he didn't deserve mercy. He wasn't sure how his father would respond: "I will go home to my father and say, 'Father, I have sinned against both heaven and you, and I am no longer worthy of being called your son. Please take me on as a hired servant.'"[5] The son's uncertainty reflects the fear we all have when we fail. Will we be rejected, unwelcome? If people really see who we are, will they still love us?

The son's fear of rejection makes the kisses of the father all the more meaningful. Without hesitating, the father releases his son from the stranglehold of judgment and shame. The kisses of the father free him to experience forgiveness, to grasp that the father has moved beyond the son's past wrongs.

The kiss of the father is one of the primary ways that we live the life of the XEALOT. It is the culmination of all our understanding, our commitment to live in a countercultural way. The kiss of the father is our readiness to forgive others, even before they ask for it. To kiss others in this way is to look beyond the mistakes and sins of the past toward a vision of what is possible through God's grace. Blessing other people — as the Father has blessed us — begins as we see God's lost and wandering sons and daughters with eyes of faith, even when they are far from home.

In all of this, we must ferociously choose to love. The kiss is not a onetime event. It's something we do again and again. We keep forgiving. We keep affirming and communicating a message of grace. We keep believing and hoping in what seems impossible. We "kiss" our sons and our daughters, our friends and our foes, even those who betray us. Kisses like this pour water into one's soul.

THE KISS OF FORGIVENESS

My own father made mistakes. However, my father had some amazing qualities as well. For example, he always tried to provide us with things he didn't have as a child. I remember days when he got up early in the morning to prepare his small steel boat to take us fishing. He would get everything ready — the fishing rods, our lunches, packing all the equipment, lifting the boat onto the car. He'd do all this preparation during the day while my brother and I were in school, so we never really saw all the effort he put into these trips. We were just excited to go fishing with Dad.

Dad took us fishing, played catch with us, swam with us; he was the all-American, perfect dad. Even when he disciplined us, he had a calm spirit, patiently asking us what we had done wrong and then meting out an appropriate punishment. When I was a child, everything seemed perfect. I felt loved and safe.

That's why it was so hard for me to discover that my dad was having an affair. I didn't want to believe it. Not *my* dad. But Mom told us that she had evidence. She had hired a detective. She had the proof. Initially, I brought this up with my father. He flatly denied it. He told me that Mom was lying. He said that he had no idea what she was talking about.

Then, one day not long after we talked, I was cleaning out my dad's truck. He had asked me to wash it and pick up a few things. As I was cleaning his floors, I found a card lying under the floor mat. He had likely forgotten that it was there. It was a card from a woman. And she wasn't my mom.

I remember walking up to my room. I was a 220-pound teenager, a football player. And I fell on my bed. I sobbed like a little baby. My father had lied to me. Suddenly, all of the fond memories I had of our times together didn't matter. I was angry. I felt betrayed. So I chose not to speak to him.

Eventually, he asked me why I wasn't talking to him. I reminded him of that day when he had asked me to wash his truck. And then I told him that I had found the card. There was silence. I'll never forget his words to me in that moment: "Well, everyone makes mistakes." I remember hearing his words, thinking about our family, and saying to myself, "That's not good enough." For the remainder of my teenage years, I avoided my father. He left our house and we had little contact. He wasn't there for the football games. He was missing when I graduated from high school. We never saw one another. And so my anger was justified.

Though I seethed with resentment and bitterness, I kept it carefully buried inside. For the most part, I didn't let my pain affect me. I went on with my life. I went to college. I was elected to a position in student government. I enjoyed a measure of popularity among the students. I was even becoming known as something of a spiritual leader on campus. Life was good.

Then, one evening, I was walking across the baseball field when it all hit me afresh. There I was, feeling successful, proud that I was leading others, when I suddenly became aware of my own hypocrisy. Hidden deep inside my heart was this deep resentment for my father, something I had never owned up to.

I felt God say to me, "Dave, you need to forgive your dad."

I quickly formulated excuses, reasons not to forgive him. "I have no feelings for him. It wouldn't be authentic. It would be lying." Then God whispered to me, without pressure or condemnation, "Do you think my Son *felt* like going to the cross?" I knew, then, what I had to do. The path of obedience was clear. I had to forgive my father.

I called him right away. He (and his new wife) was shocked to hear from me. Eventually, we set up a meeting and there was a tearful exchange of apologies. I wish I could finish this story by telling you that I had a flood of positive feelings for my dad after we reconciled. But I didn't. It took several years before the feelings came. Over time, I felt the counsel of the Holy Spirit saying two things to me: "Forgive your dad, no matter how he responds to your initiative, and remember that love is not a feeling but rather a commitment. The feelings will come in time, but love is a choice."

Over the years, my relationship with my father was restored. And through that, God graciously freed me from the stifling anger in my heart. Now I can say that I have a greater appreciation for my father. I saw him with a different set of eyes as I grew. I learned what it means to bless others, I tried to "kiss" him with the same forgiving love that God has shown to me.

As XEALOTS, countercultural followers of Christ, we know our secret weapon isn't only our academic arguments or tight syllogisms. It's not our perfectly crafted speeches. It's our radical love, a love that forgives others and serves them. Jesus argued. He taught. He preached. Yet his defining victory over evil came through an act of sacrificial love. It was a love that sacrificed, a love that opened a door for wayward sons and daughters to return home and receive the forgiveness of the Father. It was a love that made it possible for those who were far from the Father to be adopted into his family. The "kiss" of Jesus' life is evident by way of the cross. The cross was an act of loving sacrifice.

Forgiveness is the greatest miracle we experience as human beings. The healing of the sick, the crossing of the Red Sea— these pale in comparison with the miracle of forgiveness. This is because forgiveness is love in action. When we forgive, we release the offender, we accept the betrayal, and we sacrifice ourselves—our sense of entitlement—for the sake of another.

BECOMING LIKE THE FATHER

One of the most significant shifts we make as XEALOTS is the shift from *asking for* blessing to *giving* blessing, from saying "give me" to saying "use me." It's a contrarian way of being because we transition from leading to being led, from our myopic self-centeredness to others-mindedness. We have a genuine concern for others. We no longer are motivated to take what we think is ours; instead, we are free to give it all away. Instead of seeking revenge (as the father had every right to do), we embrace. We kiss. We reconcile with those who have wandered far from home.

The common trap that we fall into is becoming like the older brother in the parable. The older brother, though he has spent a lifetime with the father, doesn't share the heart of the father. He is focused on justice, on getting his share. The return of the wayward brother, far from being a reason for celebration to him, means that his inheritance will now be tapped to provide for his brother's needs as well. If you were the father, how would you respond to the older brother? With wisdom, we see the father speaking a powerful word of blessing to his older son: "Everything I have is yours."[6]

This is the truth that we need to hear when we battle our selfish tendencies: "Everything I have is yours." If we really believe this, we will be freed to live like the father, giving unconditionally, knowing that we have no need to strive or seek our own gain; everything we need is already ours. We live in the confidence that God's resources are unlimited. All that he has is ours.

Be honest with yourself. Do you believe this? Do you believe that everything God has is yours?

The apostle Paul, in his letter to the Romans, encourages us to remember what God has done for us and to have confidence that this is true. He writes, "Since he [God] did not spare even his own Son but gave him up for us all, won't he also give us everything else?"[7] If God has given us his most precious gift, his very own Son to save us, what is to keep him from giving us anything else? After all, what could God give us that is more valuable or wonderful than the gift he has already given us in Jesus? Everything else is just icing on the cake.

Do you believe that the Father has already given you all things? Or are you still looking to have your needs met? Are you still worried that you won't get your fair share of the inheritance? The love of the Father encourages us to receive his generosity. He calls us to be transformed by it. Let him kiss you over and over again!

ENCHANTED SALIVA

A friend of mine, Patricia DeWit, a XEALOT from Bangkok, Thailand, elegantly gives us a mother's perspective of the kiss. I love how she describes the kiss as "enchanted saliva."

> I remember her not so much as a university student as an enchantress. That's it. She was an enchantress disguised as a sort of half-man-half-woman who cut her own bangs, who built her own kitchen table, and who raised her own sons. The strangest things would come out of her mouth, things about which she was not self-conscious. I wondered how she could say such things and not agonize about it later. I wanted to be the woman who could talk like that and never second-guess herself.
>
> I was twenty. We were studying French. I loved the musicality of that language, the way it required you to speak from the back of your throat and the tip of your lips all at the same time. As hard as I worked that year to remember the subjunctive tense, the past participles, the gender of a noun, it has taken no effort to recall the words the Enchantress spoke to me all those years ago. She said it to all of us in that class, yet I'm convinced it was a magic spell pointed directly at me. I can't for the life of me remember her name, though I can see her face clearly, framed in

uneven chops of short tresses, a haunting openness in her eyes, and unapologetic facial hair on her upper lip.

"They say that the saliva of a woman in her childbearing years has healing properties."

Enchanted saliva.

Hmm ...

Immediately my literal creativity jumped into action and I pictured pregnant women running onto the battlefields of war, following after the cries of the wounded soldiers, cries almost too heavy in blood to lift off and be carried in the air: "Please ... spit ... I ... beg ... you ..."

Two years later I became a mother. You have no idea how much I wanted those words to be true. I guess it's all connected, on some deep-down level, to my lifelong desire to be a doctor. I love healers. Dr. Jakiew was the first healer I knew. To a five-year-old me, he was bigger than life. He wore a crisp black suit, and he smelled like a cold day. I always answered the door when he came.

I knew my way around that bag.

It was my job to carry his big black bag as he made his way into the house. I was his assistant. Boldly I rummaged in that healing bag, locating the light that would beam into our little-girl nostrils and ears and throats. I knew my way around that bag just as he knew his way around our house. As a child I realized that once Mom saw Dr. Jakiew arrive, she knew everything would be okay, and peace came, so much so that even the walls in the house calmed down. I knew I wanted to be the healing person, the doctor, who smelled of a cold day and who could calm a troubled house.

He smelled like a cold day and we knew everything would be alright.

I grew up studying the human body. No, I mean, *really* studying the human body. When I was nine years old, I enjoyed using words like *scapula* and *patella*. My favorite word was *esophagus*. I had no idea that it was pronounced "uh-SAW-faggus" and instead called it "ee-so-FA-gus." Trying to be clever, I asked my teacher in fourth grade, "Mrs. Devereaux, have you ever had a sore ee-so-FA-gus?" Is it wrong that I still find this funny?

I never did become a medical doctor, but I still wanted to be the person who could calm a troubled house. I wanted to have the ability to make everything all better. And I was still enchanted by the idea of the saliva of a woman in her childbearing years bringing healing.

Enchanted saliva; I know now what that is. It's a mother's kiss.

Since my children were born, I've smothered them in kisses. I defy their protests confidently, saying, "Your cheeks talk to me, and they tell me to kiss them." As the boys got older, I would smell them. In Thailand we have this beautiful thing called the "sniffkiss." I was always sniffing the boys. It was something they couldn't wipe off in disgust; it was more like my face hugging their face. One day, one of the boys suggested that I sniffed them because I was suspicious and really wanted to see if they'd been smoking pot.

"No!" I was insulted. "That makes me sad. I was *sniffkissing* you, loving you."

"But Mom, you sniff my hair and my shirt too, not just my face."

"I know, but there's always been something that satisfies me in the pit of my stomach when I capture the scent of my children. It's indescribable, really."

"Yeah, well, you do know, don't you, that I always wiped off your kisses?" he gloated good-naturedly.

"Yeah? Well, you do know, don't you," mocking his tone, "that it's *impossible* to wipe off a mother's kiss?"

He rolled his eyes.

"No, seriously. Didn't you ever see that episode on Discovery Channel? About mother kisses?"

"More like an episode of *Magic School Bus* and mother's *spit*, don't you think?"

"Well, Mr. Smarty Bus, I know for a *fact* that it's impossible to wipe off a mother's kiss." And here's where the words of the Enchantress came to life. "They are so indelible that they can't come off. Your wiping is actually rubbing them into your skin. And then when kids like you leave home and go off to college and cry themselves to sleep because they miss their mom, all they need to do is add a few drops of water to their cheek — or anywhere, really — because by the time they leave home their entire faces are covered in years and years and layers and layers of mother kisses, and the drops of water bring out the power of the saliva that has been lying dormant and collecting power over the years, and the mother kisses come back to life. They smell like a cold day and you feel better, and you just know that everything's going to be okay."

There was a thoughtful pause.

"And this was on the Discovery Channel?"

"Or National Geographic. I can't remember."[8]

CONCLUSION

fade

WHEN I think of John the Baptist, I imagine a guy with dread-locks wearing hippie clothing and eating locusts as snacks. He certainly didn't fit the flow of his culture. He was unorthodox, radical, earthy, and bold.

John was born in the hill country of Judah to Zechariah, a priest, and his wife, Elizabeth, (who was also of priestly lineage and related to Mary, the mother of Jesus). John spent his early years roaming the wilderness of Judea until beginning his public ministry twenty years later.

John cannot be squeezed into a mold. He had a simple message, calling those who could hear that there was someone coming—the One—and that they should get ready for his arrival. His message was simple but hard, a call to repentance. His message offended the religious. He lived as if he was part of a resistance movement.

In those days John the Baptist came to the Judean wilderness and began preaching. His message was, "Repent of your sins and turn to God, for the Kingdom of Heaven is near." The prophet Isaiah was speaking about John when he said,

> "He is a voice shouting in the wilderness,
> 'Prepare the way for the LORD's coming!
>   Clear the road for him!'"

John's clothes were woven from coarse camel hair, and he wore a leather belt around his waist. For food he ate locusts and wild honey. People from Jerusalem and from all of Judea and all over the Jordan Valley went out to see and hear John. And when they confessed their sins, he baptized them in the Jordan River.

But when he saw many Pharisees and Sadducees coming to watch him baptize, he denounced them. "You brood of snakes!" he exclaimed. "Who warned you to flee God's coming wrath? Prove by the way you live that you have repented of your sins and turned to God. Don't just say to each other, 'We're safe, for we are descendants of Abraham.' That means nothing, for I tell you, God can create children of Abraham from these very stones. Even now the ax of God's judgment is poised, ready to sever the roots of the trees. Yes, every tree that does not produce good fruit will be chopped down and thrown into the fire.

"I baptize with water those who repent of their sins and turn to God. But someone is coming soon who is greater than I am — so much greater that I'm not worthy even to be his slave and carry his sandals. He will baptize you with the Holy Spirit and with fire. He is ready to separate the chaff from the wheat with his winnowing fork. Then he will clean up the threshing area, gathering the wheat into his barn but burning the chaff with never-ending fire."[1]

John was a young man who embraced the contrarian way, living counterculturally by adopting a strict, Nazarite religious vow and remaining unshaven. His was a rebellion of a different kind. His clothing and food were simple as well. John was focused on one thing: the message God had given him to communicate. His role was simply to announce that someone greater than him was coming. A classic right-hand man.

Few people would have considered John a "successful" person. He was a man from the wilderness, uncultured and unaccustomed to the norms of society. He seemingly came out of nowhere. He proclaimed a message that rocked the

John the Baptist

establishment, offending the religious leadership and usurping their authority by acting on behalf of God. He called people to repent. He baptized them in the River Jordan. Eventually, he called out the public sin of a powerful leader. He got his head cut off. Even though he died young, John maintained the focus of his calling: lifting Christ up, pointing to him, and putting God's purposes before himself.

In his own words, John's calling in life was to eventually become irrelevant, fading from the scene. God's definition of success for John's life was for him to become unnecessary. In his own words, John makes this clear to the crowds that followed him: "You yourselves know how plainly I told you, 'I am not the Messiah. I am only here to prepare the way for him.' It is the bridegroom who marries the bride, and the best man is simply glad to stand with him and hear his vows. Therefore, I am filled with joy at his success. He must become greater and greater, and I must become less and less."[2]

The other John tells us that he is like the best man at a wedding. Though the best man plays an important part in the ceremony, it's not his wedding day. He's not the focus of attention. Instead, he fades so that the bride and the groom can shine. John's life was defined by the pursuit of irrelevance: "He must become greater ... and I must become less."

By worldly standards, John was a failure from the beginning. He lacked personal ambition. John deferred to a younger teacher, the new guy on the scene — Jesus of Nazareth. He used his own platform to promote another. He gave his own glory away. He faded into the background. Yet John was loved and respected by Jesus Christ. He did not pursue honor or glory. When Jesus spoke of John, he said, "I tell you, of all who have ever lived, none is greater than John."[3]

In many ways, Jesus takes a similar path in his own life. Jesus grows up in a no-name village. He stays out of the limelight for thirty years. He then has a short-lived, three-and-a-half-year public ministry. He dies a criminal's death by Roman crucifixion. The movement of his life is one of descension, a humble path of living for the glory of others. He ultimately defers to the Father. He says in Luke 22:42, "Father, if you are willing, please take this cup of suffering away from me. Yet I want your will to be done, not mine."

I was sharing some of this with one of our young leaders in Thailand. I could tell that he had finally caught the idea of fading into the background. Just prior to returning to the States, I met one last time with this group of young revolutionaries and asked them, "Are you guys ready to lead the way?" They shouted, "Yes!" At that moment, I was so proud of them. I knew they would take the things I had shared with them to a new level after I had left, so I said to them, "It feels so good to be unnecessary." At this, one of the young Thai leaders — feeling the weight of responsibility — said, "I can't wait to be unnecessary too."

THE MOMENT OF TRIUMPH

Charlotte's Web is a wonderful little children's story by author E. B. White about a spider named Charlotte who lives in a barn just above the stall of a pig named Wilbur. Wilbur is worried that once he grows fat enough, the farmer is going to turn him into bacon. It's a valid concern.

Charlotte and Wilbur develop a close friendship, and as Wilbur grows larger, Charlotte uses all of her resources to try to rescue Wilbur. She writes messages in her web to convince the farm's owners that Wilbur is a pig worth saving. The story builds to a final chapter titled "The Moment of Triumph."

So what was Charlotte's moment of triumph?

As the story draws to a close, Charlotte the spider is in the barn dying, and she can hear the roar of applause for Wilbur in the arena. She finds great joy in knowing that her life has meant the success of another, her close friend, Wilbur. Though no one will remember her, the things she has done and the sacrifices she has made, she is satisfied, having loved her friend in life and in death.

As I meet with followers of Christ all around the world, I see God raising up a new generation, a generation that wants to run in the footsteps of John the Baptist. A generation of nameless, faceless leaders who want to fade into the background so that Jesus will be glorified.

"He must become greater ... and I must become less."

The mission of John the Baptist is a call to each one of us, a call to a gravity-defying adventure. It's a path that frequently involves pain and struggle. It's a journey that leads us to become like the Father, to become people who bless and forgive and sacrifice ourselves for others.

It's about fading. The great ones willingly move into irrelevance.

"He must become greater ... I must become less."

EPILOGUE

Leigh, Karis, Luke, and Megan,

I love you with all my heart. This world is waiting for you to explore, inviting you to enjoy its fruit and explore the Creator behind it. I've been in this world close to fifty years now. While I'll always feel like a favored son and a rebellious kid, I love being your father. I hope you know I believe in you and am one of your biggest fans.

You live in one of the greatest transitions in human history. Our world is shifting economically, politically, technologically, and spiritually. What an exciting opportunity to create, to dream, to collaborate, and to forge new paths. I know that, as the children of a perceived leader, you have had unique challenges. You face pressures that I don't know about. But I'm confident God has designed you in the laboratory of our home. He has shaped you for a unique, promised destiny. The pain, the joy, the vision, the values, and the unusual circumstances you've experienced in Bangkok and India, in Seoul, in NYC, in Los Angeles and Europe and beyond have transformed you. You've been given the gift of global citizenship. You're third culture.

Everything is changing. This generation is hungry for God. They are hungry to experience something beyond this world. Possibilities abound in times of change. Don't get hung up on what is lost or what you may not have as you see others who have more skills or many resources. You have the Holy Spirit to fill in any gaps you think you may have. Remember that he can easily create something from nothing, just as he did in the beginning. I've seen this happen many times.

Your destiny is not about leaving a legacy; it's about flowing with the Holy Spirit. Leaving a legacy focuses on getting ready to die and passing the torch on to the next generation. Fulfilling your destiny means you have a divine purpose to joyfully pursue. This journey is mixed with joy and painful determination. The writer of Hebrews pens, "Because of the joy awaiting him, he endured the cross."[1] Joy and endurance. You're called to be liquid, to adapt.

One day Mom and I may not be around physically, but remember that you'll continue to have the Holy Spirit to guide you, comfort you, prepare the way for you, and speak to you. The Spirit will provide more than we could ever give to you. He will come alongside of you so that you are fully empowered. You may often feel ordinary, but don't forget that you have been given extraordinary favor. Your fire cannot be quenched.

So run. Eat. Enjoy. Take strolls without your shoes. Laugh hard. I mean the belly laughs that make your gut hurt. Keep the company of good friends and radical learners. Surround yourself with people who are passionate and in love with God, who strive to live in the both/and. The whole earth is your habitation. Home is wherever meaningful relationships are pursued. Kiss those who have betrayed you and forgive freely. Dare to do what is impossible. Embrace your pain as a gift. Transcend the gravity of the common life. Choose to live a supernatural life in the Spirit.

The world is looking for truth. The rawness of your humanity mixed with who you are as a child of God is a potent force. Be artfully authentic to the core. You don't have to hide. No need to fear people or ideas. Be alive with the Spirit! You will be set ablaze. The world can't help but pause when they see God in you. It's like Moses coming down off that mountain after he saw a glimpse of God. His face was glowing with light. His eyes were lit by the presence of God.

You are made to be ZEALOTS, filled with life, pursuing adventure, roaming the earth without fear. Created with some wonderful uniquenesses, you stand out in a crowd. You send spiritual tremors out every time your feet hit the ground. People won't understand you sometimes. In fact, they may turn their backs on you and think you're crazy. Don't worry, that's a good sign. If it's of God, some people won't understand. You're getting to your sweet spot in life. Be as bold as lions, unafraid to run toward your Goliaths, wearing your own armor, using your own tools to engage whatever impossible challenge may come your way. Don't get caught up in nonessentials, but stay focused on what is important. Find God in the margins and discover those on the fringe; they will lead the revolutions that change the world. Love silence and solitude; it will be your perpetual fountain of refreshment and refinement, a spiritual reservoir of cold springwater. Be transparent and honest. Pursue intimacy with those you are called to love. The nations are your playground; find your tribe. You don't need many. But those in your clan love with all your heart. Every place you step is God's ground. Our world is a village that continues to grow smaller. Lean into the Holy Spirit; he is there to comfort, guide, protect, inspire, and empower you. Be fully awake to this unique moment in history. He's in you, ready to unleash his beauty.

Defy the normal. Be naturally supernatural. It's your destiny. You're a XEALOT.

All my love,
Dad

NOTES

Introduction

1. For background music while you read this section, check out the song "Uprising" by Muse: *http://www.youtube.com /watch?v=w8KQmps-Sog.*

Part 1: Mind

1. Rom. 12:1 – 2.

Chapter 1: Zombies

1. John 1:46 (my paraphrase).
2. Ps. 118:22 – 23.
3. Consider Moses in Exodus 3, for example.
4. 1 Cor. 1:27.

Chapter 2: Chuang Tzu

1. Prov. 4:23.
2. Thomas Merton, *The Way of Chuang Tzu* (1965; New York: New Directions, 1969), 110 – 11. "The Woodcarver" by Thomas Merton, from *The Way of Chuang Tzu*, copyright ©1965 by The Abbey of Gethsemani. Reprinted by permission of New Directions Publishing Corp.
3. Exod. 3:11.
4. If you're ready to give fasting a try, check out *http://globalfast.org.* You can make a difference while you're fasting.

Chapter 3: Success

1. Mark 8:35–37.
2. Judg. 7:1–7.
3. 2 Sam. 23:8.
4. Scot McKnight, *One.Life: Jesus Calls, We Follow* (Grand Rapids, Mich.: Zondervan, 2010), 31.
5. 1 Cor. 3:5–9.
6. 1 Cor. 1:27.
7. Mark 10:45.
8. John 21:18.
9. Mark 8:36.
10. 1 Cor. 1:18–31.
11. 2 Cor. 12:10.
12. For more information about the work of Tara Russell, check out *www.createcommongood.org*.

Chapter 4: Scars

1. Ps. 139:12.
2. John 12:25–26.
3. 2 Cor. 12:7–10.
4. Ps. 23:5.
5. 1 Cor. 15:51–58.

Chapter 5: Mystery

1. 1 Cor. 2:4 (NIV).
2. Ps. 119:9.
3. Rom. 8:26.
4. 1 Peter 1:8.
5. Isa. 40:31.
6. 2 Tim. 3:16.
7. James 2:17.

Chapter 6: Obedience

1. Ps. 51:16–17.
2. Matt. 5:44.
3. Rom. 12:14.
4. Matt. 22:39.

5. Mark 8:34.

6. John 15:19.

7. Luke 6:37.

Chapter 7: Supernaturally Natural

1. Eccl. 3:11.

2. 2 Tim. 1:7.

3. John 7:37–39.

4. Matt. 7:14.

5. 2 Tim. 3:5.

6. Joel 2:28–29.

7. Acts 2:1–7, 12–13 (emphases added).

8. 1 Cor. 14:33.

9. 1 Cor. 14:40.

Chapter 8: Becoming a Father

1. Luke 15:11–32.

2. Ps. 139:17–18.

3. Ps. 139:1–4.

4. Luke 15:20.

5. Luke 15:18–19.

6. Luke 15:31.

7. Rom. 8:32.

8. Patricia DeWit, "Enchanted Saliva," *Patridew's Perfect World*, May 3, 2011, *http://patridew.wordpress.com/2011/05/03/enchanted-saliva/*. Used with permission.

Conclusion

1. Matt. 3:1–12.

2. John 3:28–30.

3. Luke 7:28.

Epilogue

1. Heb. 12:2.

The Monkey and the Fish

Liquid Leadership for a Third-Culture Church

Dave Gibbons

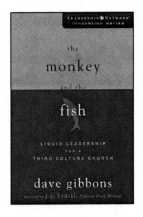

Our world is marked by unprecedented degrees of multiculturalism, ethnic diversity, social shifts, international collaboration, and technology-driven changes. The changes are profound, especially when you consider the unchecked decline in the influence, size, and social standing of the church. There is an undercurrent of anxiety in the evangelical world, and a hunger for something new. And we're sensing the urgency of it.

We need fresh, creative counterintuitive ways of doing ministry and leading the church in the twenty-first century. We need to adapt. Fast. Both in our practices and our thinking.

The aim of this book is simple: When we understand the powerful forces at work in the world today, we'll learn how something called the Third Culture can yield perhaps the most critical missing ingredient in the church today—adaptability—and help the church remain on the best side of history.

A Third Culture church and a Third Culture leader look at our new global village and the church's role in that village in a revolutionary way. It's a way to reconnect with the historical roots of what Jesus envisioned the church could be—a people known for a brand of love, unity, goodness, and extravagant spirit that defies all conventions.

This book is part of the successful Leadership Innovation Series.

For purchase information, sample chapters and author videos visit
www.Zondervan.com/LNIS

DISCOVER YOUR DESTINY!
BECOME A **XEALOT** NOW!

All of **XEALOT'S** creative offerings include helping people to discover their destiny and customizing development according to one's learning style. Each of our program offerings includes our unique focus on east/west cultural relationships, creativity, the **XEALOT** way, global leaders from multiple domains of society and seeing pain/struggle as part of our destiny.

XEALOT PREMIUM CONTENT

Visit Xealot.net/premium to access a **FREE trial offer** of XEALOT content including multimedia, assessment tools and further insights from Dave Gibbons and other XEALOT guides.
Use special access code: DESTINY

XEALOT TRIBES

XEALOT Tribes is a cohort model that meets 3 times a year in a small setting. This 1 year activist oriented intensive and concentrated time is designed for a small circle of creatives, innovators and entrepreneurs.

XEALOT COMMUNITAS

Small to mid-size groups that meet more regularly than XEALOT Tribes and are part of existing organizations. XEALOT Communitas is missional living found within existing networks like companies, organic groups, clubs or among friends.

BEGIN THE ADVENTURE AT XEALOT.NET OR CONTACT US AT XEALOT@XEALOT.NET

XEALOT
D E S T I N Y

MUTANTS. OUTSIDERS. FRINGE. THIS IS XEALOT.

XEALOT is a human development group focusing on helping Creatives, Innovators, and Artists find their destiny. We equip and resource these individuals to live out their destiny through XEALOT learning styles. Our life-changing process emphasizes struggle and strengths, east/west cultural relationships, and customized, holistic development. Contact us at Xealot@Xealot.net or visit our site at XEALOT.net.

FOLLOW US

Los Angeles · New York · Bangkok · Seoul · Sao Paulo · Mexico City

Share Your Thoughts

With the Author: Your comments will be forwarded to the author when you send them to *zauthor@zondervan.com*.

With Zondervan: Submit your review of this book by writing to *zreview@zondervan.com*.

Free Online Resources at
www.zondervan.com

Zondervan AuthorTracker: Be notified whenever your favorite authors publish new books, go on tour, or post an update about what's happening in their lives at www.zondervan.com/authortracker.

Daily Bible Verses and Devotions: Enrich your life with daily Bible verses or devotions that help you start every morning focused on God. Visit www.zondervan.com/newsletters.

Free Email Publications: Sign up for newsletters on Christian living, academic resources, church ministry, fiction, children's resources, and more. Visit www.zondervan.com/newsletters.

Zondervan Bible Search: Find and compare Bible passages in a variety of translations at www.zondervanbiblesearch.com.

Other Benefits: Register yourself to receive online benefits like coupons and special offers, or to participate in research.

ZONDERVAN®

ZONDERVAN.com/
AUTHORTRACKER
follow your favorite authors